The *Izumi Shikibu nikki*

HEIAN COURT HEROINES

The *Izumi Shikibu nikki*

Izumi Shikibu

Translated by
ANNIE SHEPLEY ŌMORI AND KŌCHI DOI

Revised and Edited by
WILLIAM DE LANGE

First edition, 2019

Originally published in *Diaries of Court Ladies of Old Japan*

Published by TOYO PRess
Visit us at: **www.toyopress.com**

Copyright © 2019 TOYO PRess

All rights reserved. No part of this publication may be reproduced, stored or introduced into a retrieval system, or transmitted, in any form or by any means (electronic, mechanical, photocopying, recording or otherwise), without the prior written permission of both the copyright owner and the above publisher of this book.

ISBN 978-94-92722-225

Introduction

The Japanese have a convenient method of calling their historical periods by the names of the places which were the seats of government while they lasted. The first of these epochs of real importance is the Nara period, which began A.D. 710 and endured until 794; all before that may be classed as archaic. Previous to the Nara period, the Japanese had been a semi-nomadic race. As each successive emperor came to the throne, he built himself a new palace, and founded a new capital. There had been more than sixty capitals before the Nara period. Such shifting was not conducive to the development of literature and the arts, and it was not until a permanent government was established at Nara that these began to flourish. This is scarcely the place to trace the history of Japanese literature, but fully to understand these charming diaries of court ladies of old Japan, it is necessary to know a little of the world they lived in, to be able to feel their atmosphere and recognize their allusions.

We know a good deal about Japan today, but the Japan with which we are familiar only slightly resembles that of the diaries. Centuries of feudalism, of Dark Ages, have come between. We must go behind all this and begin again. We have all heard of the Forty-seven *Rōnin* and the *nō* drama, of *shōgun*, *daimyō*, and *samurai*, and many of us live in daily communion with Japanese prints. It gives us pause to reflect that the earliest of these things is almost as many centuries ahead of the ladies as it is behind us. *Shōgun* means simply "general," and of course there were always generals, but the power of the *shōgun*, and the military feudalism of which the *daimyō* and their attendant *samurai* were a part, did not really begin until the middle of the twelfth century and did not reach its full development until the middle of the fourteenth. The *nō* drama started with the ancient religious pantomimic dance, the *kagura*, but not until words were added in the fourteenth century did it be-

INTRODUCTION

come the *nō*. Similarly, block color printing was first practised in 1695, while such famous print artists as Utamaro, Hokusai, and Hiroshige are all products of the eighteenth or early nineteenth centuries. To find the ladies behind the dark military ages, we must go back a long way, even to the century before their own, and so gain a sort of perspective for them and their time.

Chinese literature and civilization were introduced into Japan somewhere between 270 and 310 AD, and Buddhism followed in 552. Of course, all such dates must be taken with a certain degree of latitude; Oriental historians are anything but precise in these matters. Chinese influence and Buddhism are the two enormous facts to be reckoned with in understanding Japan, and considering what an effect they have had, it is not a little singular that Japan has always been able to preserve her native character. To be sure, Shintōism was never displaced by Buddhism, but the latter made a tremendous appeal to the Japanese temperament, as the diaries show. In fact, it was not until the Meiji period (1867-1912) that Shintōism was again made the state religion. With the introduction of Chinese civilization came the art of writing, when is not accurately known, but printing from movable blocks followed from Korea in the eighth century. As was inevitable under the circumstances, Chinese came to be considered the language of learning. Japanese scholars wrote in Chinese. All the "serious" books—history, theology, science, law—were written in Chinese as a matter of course. But, in 712, a volume called *Kojiki*, or *Records of Ancient Matters*, was compiled in the native tongue. It is the earliest book in Japanese now extant.

If the scholars wrote in a borrowed language, the poets knew better. They wrote in their own, and the poetry of the Nara period has been preserved for us in an anthology, the *Manyōshū* or *Collection of Ten Thousand Leaves*. This was followed at the beginning of the tenth century by the *Kokinshū*, the *Collection from Ancient and Modern Times*, to which the editor, Tsurayuki, felt obliged to write a Chinese preface. The ladies of the diaries were extremely familiar with these volumes, their own writings are full of allusions to poems contained in them. Sei Shōnagon, writing early in the eleventh century, describes a young lady's education as consisting of writing, music, and the twenty volumes of the *Kokinshū*. So it came about that while learned gentlemen still continued to write in Chinese, poetry, fiction, di-

INTRODUCTION

aries, and desultory essays called *zuihitsu* (following the pen) were written in Japanese.

Now the position of women at this time was very different from what it afterwards became in the feudal period. The Chinese called Japan the "Empress Country," because of the ascendancy which women enjoyed there. They were educated, they were allowed a share of inheritance, and they had their own houses. It is an extraordinary and important fact that much of the best literature of Japan has been written by women. Three of these most remarkable women are the authors of the diaries; a fourth to be named with them, Sei Shōnagon, to whom I have just referred, was a contemporary.

In 794, the capital was moved from Nara to Kyoto, which was given the name of Heian-kyō or "City of Peace," and with the removal, a new period, the Heian, began. It lasted until 1186, and our ladies lived in the very middle of it.

By this time Japan was thoroughly civilized; she was, indeed, a little over-civilized, a little too fined down and delicate. At least this is true of all that life which centered round the court at Heian-kyō. To historians the Heian period represents the rise and fall of the Fujiwara family. This powerful family had served the emperors from time out of mind as heads of the Shintō priests, and after the middle of the seventh century, they became ministers or prime ministers. An immense clan, they gradually absorbed all the civil offices in the kingdom, while the military offices were filled by the Taira and Minamoto clans. It was the rise of these last as the Fujiwara declined that eventually led to the rule of the *shōgun* and the long centuries of feudalism and civil war.

But in the middle of the Heian period the Fujiwara were very much everywhere. Most of those court ladies who were the authors of remarkable books were the daughters of governors of provinces, and that meant Fujiwaras to a greater or lesser degree. At that time polygamy flourished in Japan, and the family had grown to a prodigious size. Since a civil office meant a post for a Fujiwara, many of them were happily provided for, but they were so numerous that they outnumbered the legitimate positions and others had to be created to fill the demand. The court was full of persons of both sexes holding sinecures, with a great deal of time on their hands and nothing to do in it but write poetry—which they did exceedingly well—and attend the various functions

INTRODUCTION

prescribed by etiquette. Ceremonials were many and magnificent, and poetry writing became not only a game but a natural adjunct to every possible event.

The Japanese as a people are dowered with a rare and exquisite taste, and in the Heian period taste was cultivated to an amazing degree. Murasaki Shikibu records the astounding pitch to which it had reached in a passage in her diary. Speaking of the emperor's ladies at a court festivity, she says of the dress of one of them:

> One had a little fault in the color combination at the wrist opening. When she went before the royal presence to fetch something, the nobles and high officials noticed it. Afterwards Lady Saisho regretted it deeply. It was not so bad—only one color was a little too pale.

That passage needs no comment; it is completely illuminating. It is a paraphrase of the whole era.

Heian-kyō was a little city, long one way by some seventeen thousand odd feet, or about three and a third miles, wide the other by fifteen thousand, or approximately another three miles, and it is doubtful if the space within the city wall was ever entirely covered by houses. The palace was built in the so-called Azumaya style, a form of architecture also followed in noblemen's houses. The roof, or rather roofs, for there were many buildings, was covered with bark, and, inside, the divisions into rooms were made by different sorts of moving screens. At the period of the diaries, the reigning emperor, Ichijō, had two wives: Sadako, the first empress (*kōgō*), was the daughter of a previous prime minister, Michitaka, a Fujiwara, of course; the other, Akiko, daughter of Michinaga, the prime minister of the diaries and a younger brother of Michitaka, was second empress (*chūgū*). These empresses each occupied a separate house in the palace. Kokiden was the name of empress Sadako's house; Fujitsubō the name of Empress Akiko's. The rivalry between these ladies was naturally great, and extended even to their entourage. Each strove to surround herself with ladies who were not only beautiful, but learned. The bright star of Empress Sadako's court was Sei Shōnagon, the author of a remarkable book, the *Makura no sōshi* or *Pillow Sketches*, while Murasaki Shikibu held the same exalted position in Empress Akiko's court.

INTRODUCTION

We are to imagine a court founded upon the Chinese model, but not nearly so elaborate. A brilliant assemblage of persons all playing about a restricted but very bright centre. From it, the high officials went out to be governors of distant provinces, and the lesser ones followed them to minor posts, but in spite of the distinction of such positions, distance and the inconvenience of travelling made the going a sort of laurelled banishment. These gentlemen left Heian-kyō with regret and returned with satisfaction. But the going, and the years of residence away, was one of the commonplaces of social life. Fujiwara though one might be, one often had to wait and scheme for an office, and the diaries contain more than one reference to such waiting and the bitter disappointment when the office was not up to expectation.

These functionaries travelled with a large train of soldiers and servants, but, with the best will in the world, these last could not make the journeys other than tedious and uncomfortable. Still there were alleviations, because of the very taste of which I have spoken. The scenery was often beautiful, and whether the traveller were the governor himself or his daughter, he noticed and delighted in it.

The *Sarashina nikki*, for instance, is full of this appreciation of nature. We are told of "a very beautiful beach with long-drawn white waves," of a torrent whose water was "white as if thickened with rice flour." We need only think of the prints with which we are familiar to be convinced of the accuracy of this picture:

> The waves of the outer sea were very high, and we could see them through the pine-trees which grew scattered over the sandy point that stretched between us and the sea. They seemed to strike across the ends of the pine branches and shone like jewels.

The diarist goes on to remark that "it was an interesting sight," which we can very well believe, since certainly she makes us long to see it.

These journeys were mostly made on horseback, but there were other methods of progression, which were probably not always feasible for long distances. The nobles used various kinds of carriages drawn by one bullock, and there were also palanquins carried by bearers.

It was not only the officials who made journeys, all the

INTRODUCTION

world made them, to temples and shrines for the good of their souls. There are religious yearnings in all the diaries, and many emperors and gentlemen entered the priesthood, Michinaga among them. *Sūtra* recitation and incantation were ceaselessly performed at court. We can gain some idea of the almost fanatical hold which Buddhism had over the educated mind by the fact that the Fujiwara family built such great temples as Gokuraku-ji, Hōkō-in, Jōmyō-ji, Muryōju-ji, etc. It is recorded that emperor Shirakawa, at a date somewhat subsequent to the diaries, made pilgrimages four times to Kumano, and during his visits there "worshipped 5470 painted Buddhas, 127 carved Buddhas sixteen feet high, 3150 Buddhas lifesized, 2930 carved Buddhas shorter than three feet, 21 pagodas, 446,630 miniature pagodas." A busy man truly, but the record does not mention what became of the affairs of state meanwhile. That this worship was by no means lip-devotion merely, any reader of the *Sarashina nikki* can see. That it was mixed with much superstition and a profound belief in dreams is also abundantly evident. But let us, for a moment, recollect the time. It will place the marvel of this old, careful civilization before us as nothing else can.

To be sure, Greece and Rome had been, but they had passed away, or at least their greatness had gone and apparently left no trace. While these Japanese ladies were writing, Europe was in the full blackness of her darkest ages. Germany was founding the "Holy Roman Empire of the German Nation," characteristically founding it with the mailed fist. Moorish civilization was at its height in Spain. Robert Capet was king of poor famine-scourged France. Ethelred the Unready was ruling in England and doing his best to keep off the Danes by payment and massacre. Later, while the *Sarashina nikki* was being written, emperor Canute was sitting in his armchair and giving orders to the sea. Curious, curious world! So far apart from the one of the diaries. And to think that even five hundred years later Columbus was sending letters into the interior of Cuba, addressed to the Emperor of Japan!

These diaries show us a world extraordinarily like our own, if very unlike in more than one important particular. The noblemen and women of Emperor Ichijō's court were poets and writers of genius, their taste as a whole has never been surpassed by any people at any time, but their scientific knowledge was elementary in the extreme. Diseases

INTRODUCTION

and conflagrations were frequent. In a space of fifty-one years, the royal palace burnt down eleven times. During the same period, there were four great pestilences, a terrible drought, and an earthquake. Robbers infested many parts of the countryside, and were a constant fear to travellers and pilgrims. Childbirth was very dangerous. The scene of the birth of a child to Empress Akiko, with which Murasaki Shikibu's diary begins, shows us all its bitter horror. From page to page we share the writer's suspense, and with our greater knowledge, it is with a sense of wonder that we watch the empress's return to health.

Diseases and conflagrations are seldom more than episodes in a normal life lived under sane conditions, and it is because these diaries reflect the real life of these three ladies that they are important. The world they portray is in most ways quite as advanced as our own, and in some, much more so. Rice was the staple of food, and although Buddhistic sentiment seldom permitted people to eat the flesh of animals, they had an abundance of fish, which was eaten boiled, baked, raw, and pickled. There was no sugar, but cakes were made of fruit and nuts, and there was always rice wine or *sake*. Gentlefolk usually dressed in silk. They wore many layers of colored silk garments, and delighted in the harmony produced by the color combinations, or of a bright lining subdued by the tone of an outer robe. The ladies all painted their faces, and the whole toilet was a matter of sufficient moment to raise it into a fine art. Many of these lovely dresses are described by Murasaki Shikibu:

> The beautiful shape of their hair, tied with ribbons, was like that of the beauties in Chinese pictures. Lady Saemon held the emperor's sword. She wore a blue-green patternless *karaginu* and shaded train with floating bands and belt of floating thread brocade dyed in dull red. Her outer robe was trimmed with five folds and was chrysanthemum colored. The glossy silk was of crimson. Her figure and movement, when we caught a glimpse of it, was flower-like and dignified. Lady Ben no Naishi held the box of the emperor's seals. Her *uchigi* was grape-colored. She is a very small and smile-giving person and seems shy and I was sorry for her.... Her hair bands were blue-green. Her appearance suggested one of the ancient dream maidens descended from heaven.

INTRODUCTION

A little later she tells us that "the beaten stuffs were like the mingling of dark and light maple leaves in autumn." Describing in some detail the festivity at which these ladies appeared, she makes the comment that "only the right bodyguard wore clothes of shrimp pink." To one in love with color, these passages leave a deep nostalgia for such a bright and sophisticated court.

And everywhere, everywhere, there is poetry. A gentleman hands a lady a poem on the end of his fan and she is expected to reply in kind within the instant. Poems form an important part in the ritual of betrothal. A daughter of good family never allowed herself to be seen by men—a custom that appears to have admitted many exceptions. A man would write a poetical love letter to the lady of his choice which she must answer amiably, even should she have no mind to him. If she were happily inclined, he would visit her secretly at night and leave before daybreak. He would then write again, following which she would give a banquet and introduce him to her family. After this, he could visit her openly, although she would still remain for some time in her father's house. This custom of love letter writing and visiting is shown in Izumi Shikibu's diary.

Obviously the poems were short, and here, in order to understand those in the text, it may be well to consider for a moment in what Japanese poetry consists.

Japanese is a syllabic language like our own, but, unlike our own, it is not accented. Also, every syllable ends with a vowel, the consequence being that there are only five rhymes in the whole language. Since the employment of so restricted a rhyme scheme would be unbearably monotonous, the Japanese hit upon the happy idea of counting syllables. Our metrical verse also counts syllables, but we combine them into different kinds of accented feet. Without accent, this was not possible, so the Japanese poet limits their number and uses them in a pattern of alternating lines. Their prosody is based upon the numbers five and seven, a five-syllable line alternating with one of seven syllables, with, in some forms, two seven-syllable lines together at the end of a period, in the manner of our couplet. The favorite form, the *tanka*, is in thirty-one syllables, and runs five, seven, five, seven, seven. There is a longer form, the *nagauta*, but it has never been held in as high favor. The poems in the diaries are all *tanka* in the original. It can be seen that much cannot be said in so confined a medium,

INTRODUCTION

but much can be suggested, and it is just in this art of suggestion that the Japanese excel. The *hokku* is an even briefer form. In it, the concluding hemistich of the *tanka* is left off, and it is just in his hemistich that the meaning of the poem is brought out, so that the *hokku* is a mere essence—a whiff of an idea to be created in full by the hearer. But the *hokku* was not invented until the fifteenth century. Before that, the *tanka*, in spite of occasional attempts to vary it by adding more lines, changing their order, using the pattern in combination as a series of stanzas, reigned supreme, and it is still the chief classic form for all Japanese poetry.

One of the strangest and most interesting things about the diaries is that their authors were such very different kinds of people. Izumi Shikibu is as unlike Murasaki Shikibu as could well happen. She is as different as the most celebrated poet of her time is likely to be from the most celebrated novelist, for she is the greatest woman poet Japan has had. The author of seven volumes of poems, this diary is the only prose writing of hers that is known. It is an intimate account of a love affair that seems to have been more than usually passionate and pathetic. Passionate, provocative, enchanting, it is evident that Izumi Shikibu could never have been the discriminating observer, the critic of manners, Murasaki Shikibu became. Life was powerless to mellow so vivid a personality. But neither could it subdue it. She gives us no suggestion of resignation. She lived intensely, as her diary shows; she always had done so, and doubtless she always did. We see her as untamable, a genius compelled to follow her inclinations. Difficult to deal with, maybe, but like strong wine, wonderfully stimulating.

Izumi Shikibu was born in 974. She was the eldest daughter of Ōe Masamune, another governor of Echizen. In 995, she married Tachibana Michisada, governor of Izumi, hence her name. From this gentleman she was divorced, but just when we do not know, and he died shortly after, probably during the great pestilence that played such havoc throughout Japan and in which Murasaki Shikibu's husband had also died. Her daughter, who followed in her mother's footsteps as a poet, had been born in 997.

But Izumi Shikibu was too fascinating and too petulant to nurse her disappointment in a chaste seclusion. She became the mistress of prince Tametaka, who died in 1002. It is very soon after this event that the diary begins. Her new

INTRODUCTION

lover was prince Atsumichi, and the diary seems to have been written solely to appease her mind, and to record the poems that passed between them and which Izumi Shikibu evidently regarded as the very essence of their souls.

In the beginning, the affair was carried on with the utmost secrecy, but clandestine meetings could not satisfy the lovers, and at last the prince persuaded her to take up her residence in the palace as one of his ladies. Considering the manners of the time, it is a little puzzling to see why there should have been such an outcry at this, but outcry there certainly was. The princess took violent umbrage at the prince's proceeding and left the palace on a long visit to her relations.

So violent grew the protestations in the little world of the court that, in 1004, Izumi Shikibu left the palace and separated herself entirely from the prince. It was probably to emphasize the definiteness of the separation that, immediately after her departure, she married Fujiwara no Yasumasa, governor of Tango, and left with him for that province in 1005. The facts bear out this supposition, but we do not know it from her own lips, as the diary breaks off soon after she moves to the palace.

In 1008, she was summoned back to Heian-kyō to serve the empress in the same court where Murasaki Shikibu had been since 1005. Whatever effect the scandal may have had four years earlier, her receiving the post of lady-in-waiting proves it to have been worth forgetting in view of her fame, and Empress Akiko must have rejoiced to add this celebrated poet to her already remarkable bevy of ladies. Of course there was jealousy—who can doubt it? No reader of the diaries can imagine that Izumi Shikibu and Murasaki Shikibu can have been sympathetic, and we must take with a grain of salt the latter's caustic comment:

> Lady Izumi Shikibu corresponds charmingly, but her behavior is improper indeed. She writes with grace and ease and a flashing wit. There is a fragrance even in her smallest words. Her poems are attractive, but mere improvisations that drop from her mouth spontaneously. Every one of them has some interesting point, and she is acquainted with ancient literature too. But she is not like a true artist filled with the genuine spirit of poetry, and I think even she cannot presume to pass judgment on the poems of others.

INTRODUCTION

Is it possible that Izumi Shikibu had been so rash as to pass judgment on some of Murasaki Shikibu's efforts?

Of course it is beyond the power of any translation to preserve the full effect of the original, but even in translation, Izumi Shikibu's poems are singularly beautiful and appealing. In her own country, they are considered never to have been excelled in freshness and freedom of expression. There is something infinitely sad in the following poem, which she is said to have written on her death-bed, as the end of a passionate life:

> *Out of the dark,*
> *Into a dark path*
> *I now must enter:*
> *Shine on me from afar*
> *Moon of the mountain fringe.*[1]

Amy Lowell

Tachibana

I had spent many months lamenting the passing of my love, the late prince Tametaka.[2] Life to me seemed more shadowy than a dream. Already the tenth day of April, the Month of Deutzia, was over. A deeper shade lay under the trees and the grass on the embankment was greener.[3] These changes, unnoticed by most, seemed beautiful to me, and while musing on them a man stepped lightly along behind the hedge. I was idly curious, but when he neared I recognized the page of the late prince.

The page came at a sorrowful moment, so I said, "Where have you been all this time? You seem to me now an acquaintance of a distant past."

"Forgive me for not visiting you," said the youth, "but I

though it presumptuous to assume such familiarity—you see, I have been on a pilgrimage to mountain temples as of late. Yet even so, I felt forlorn and idle without my lord, and thus I entered instead the service of his younger brother, Prince Atsumichi."[4]

"Excellent! Prince Atsumichi is very elegant, but I hear he is distant and aloof. I suppose you cannot serve him with the same freedom as you did his older brother?"

"No," he replied, "but he is very gracious. He asked me whether I ever visit you nowadays. 'Yes, I do,' I said. Then, breaking off this branch of *tachibana*, his highness replied, 'Give this to her, see how she will like them.'"

The prince must have had in mind the old poem:

> *The scent of the* tachibana *in May*
> *Recalls the perfumed sleeves*
> *Of him who is no longer here.*

"Well, I'll be on my way again," said the youth, "what shall I say to the prince?"

Thinking it rude to return an oral message through a page, I replied, "Since your new lord has no reputation yet for being capricious, he won't mind me sending him word in the form of a poem," and I wrote it down in a letter:

That scent, indeed,
brings distant memories
But rather, to be reminded of that other,
Would I hear the hototogisu*'s song.*[5]

Prince Atsumichi stood restlessly on the edge of the veranda, when he spotted the youth in the shadow, clearly burdened with something on his mind. "How now?" he said, and the youth finally came forward and handed him my letter. The prince read it and wrote this answer:

Perched on the same branch
The hototogisu *sings*
With voice unchanged,
That you shall know.

Handing his reply to the page, the prince went inside, saying, "Speak to no one of this, lest I be considered an amorous man."

The page brought the poem to me. "Wonderful!" I said. And I thought to myself, *I will reply in this fashion whenever I receive such letters*, though I did not immediately do so.

Yet the prince, having received only one letter, immediately sat down to compose another:

> *To you I betrayed my heart—*
> *Alas! Confessing*
> *Brings deeper grief,*
> *I lament this day.*

Not being of a prudent disposition myself, and keenly feeling the absence of a man in my life, I was captivated by his letter and replied:

> *If you lament this single day*
> *In your heart of hearts*
> *Consider all the sorrow*
> *That has passed through mine*
> *Since the passing of you brother.*

The Tryst

In this way the prince often sent me letters, and I—though occasionally—replied, and spent my days feeling my loneliness a little assuaged.

Again there was a letter from the prince, and it seemed its lines were filled with more feeling than usual:

> *I would solace you with consoling words*
> *If spoken in vain*
> *No longer could be exchanged.*

Were we to meet in private, we could reminisce about my departed brother, and I could perhaps console you. What if we were to meet in secret this evening?

I replied:

> *Hearing of comfort*
> *I wish to talk with you,*
> *Yet like a submerged common weed,*
> *Steeped in sorrow I am,*
> *So what's the use?*[6]

The prince thought, *I will surprise her with my visit.* Busying himself from noon onward in preparation for the tryst, he called to his side Ukon no Jō,[7] who had recently acted as an intermediary, and said "Prepare my carriage. I intend to go out in secret."

Thinking, *He will be visiting that woman Shikibu*, Ukon no Jō accompanied the prince, who did not want to attract attention, and took a plain and undecorated carriage.

When they arrived and the intermediary announced, "The prince has come to see her ladyship," I was deeply embarrassed, though I could not tell my servant to say I was not in. *Only this noon I wrote to him*, I thought, *so to send him away now, while I am at home, would seem heartless.*

And so, thinking, *I will just talk to him for a while*, I

THE IZUMI SHIKIBU NIKKI

placed a cushion by the west doors of the pavilion, and invited the prince in. Was it because he was so much admired by the world that he seemed to me unusually fascinating? My heart was captivated by his beauty, and while we were talking the moon came out, almost blinding us with its brightness.

Then he said, "As I have been out of society and living in the shade, I am not used to meet in such a conspicuous place as this—I feel so embarrassed! "Let me come in where you are sitting. Observe my conduct from now onwards and you will see that it is not the kind of conduct you may have observed in the men you have met thus far."

"How odd!" I said. "I merely though of spending an evening in conversation, yet here you are, speaking words like 'from now onwards.'" Thus it grew late as we rambled on incoherently.

Are we thus to spend the night to no purpose? the prince though, and asked:

> *Were the night to pass,*
> *Without even the faintest dream—*
> *What shall remain to me of this summer night?*

I replied,

> *Thinking of the world*
> *Sleeves moist with tears are my bedfellows.*
> *Calmly to dream sweet dreams—*
> *There is no night for that.*

Let alone a night to spend with you.

Refusing to yield he replied, "My station isn't such that I can leave the palace easily. You may think me impudent in saying so, but the way my feelings for you are stirring in me is truly frightening!" And having said so he suddenly ducked under the bamboo blinds and slipped inside.

Thus we spent the night together, whispering ardent promises to each other until dawn broke and the prince left.

No sooner had he returned to the palace than he sent me a letter, saying:

How are you feeling? As for me, I am thinking of you all the time.

He had added:

> *To you it may be a commonplace*
> *To speak of love,*
> *But my feelings this morning—*
> *To nothing can compare!*

I replied:

> *Whether commonplace or not—*
> *To me it feels not so,*
> *For this morning I know the pangs of love.*

Having thus written my reply I thought, *What a strange person am I! I whom the late price loved so dearly.* And I was sad and disturbed with these thoughts.

It was at this juncture that the page came round. I though, *Is he bringing a letter from the prince for me?* but he wasn't, and I though, *How lamentable!* But then I reflected it was lewd of me to think in this manner.

When the page returned to the palace, I entrusted him with another letter:

THE IZUMI SHIKIBU NIKKI

How my heart aches for your arrival!
This morning's parting
Weighs heavily on my heart
Without even a letter to relieve it.

The prince read the letter and thought, *She is really hurting*, but immediately realized he could not continue to keep up these visits. *My legal wife, the princess,[8] being a nobleman's daughter, is unlikely to ever be the typical harmonious spouse. Yet she will surely grow suspicious of my nightly excursions. Moreover*, he though, *it is because of this very same woman that my older brother was criticized untill his dying day.* And thus, being tormented by these emotions, the prince's affection for me was less deep than it might have been.

But that evening another letter came:

Had you said
You were waiting for me
With all your heart,
Without a moment's pause
towards the house of my beloved
Should I have sped!

When I think how lightly you may regard me!

I immediately answered:

Why should I think lightly of you?

> *A drop of dew I am*
> *Hanging from a leaf*
> *Yet not unrestful,*
> *For on this branch*
> *I seem to have existed*
> *From before the birth of earth.*

Please think of me as like the drop of dew that cannot live unless the leaf supports it.

The prince received the letter. He wanted to come, but being inexperienced in matters of love, he hesitated and several days went by without us seeing each other.

The Pine Wood Door

When the last day of April had finally arrived I wrote:

If today passes
Your muffled voice of April, O hototogisu[10]
When will I hear you?

I sent the poem to the palace, but since Prince Atsumichi had so many callers he did not have time. But the next morning, when the page presented the letter, he wrote:

The hototogisu*'s song in spring is full of pain.*
Listen and you will hear his song of summer
Full-throated as of today.

And so he came at last, avoiding the public gaze. I was readying myself to visit the temple, and spending the day in religious abstinence. And believing the prince harbored no particular affection for me, we spent the night with me pretending to be absorbed in religious services and not paying him much attention.

In the morning the prince said, "I have spent a very strange night"—

> *New such feelings are for me:*
> *We have been close,*
> *Yet spent the night not meeting.*

And he added, "I am wretched."
If felt his distress and was sorry for him, and said:

> *With endless sorrow*
> *My heart is weighted*
> *And night after night is passed*
> *Without my eyelids meeting.*

For me this is not new.

THE IZUMI SHIKIBU NIKKI

The next day, the prince wrote to me, saying:

Will you visit the temple today? When shall you be at home again? I am more anxious than ever too see you.

I answered:

*In its season the time of gently falling rain will be over.
Likewise my sorrow will vanish with the passing of time.
Yet your longing has upset my heart.
Will we meet again tonight?*

This much you made me feel—so much so, I even thought of abandoning my temple visit.

Having dispatched the letter I went on my pilgrimage. I arrived home three days later to find a letter from him:

My heart yearns for you, and I wish to see you, yet when I think of the way you treated me the other night I feel annoyed and discouraged, and it feels as if we had become terribly estranged:

She is cold-hearted,
Yet I cannot forget her.
Time wipes out bitterness,
But deepens longing
Which today have overcome me.

How much, I wonder, are you aware of my deepest feelings for you.

I replied:

Are you coming?
Scarcely believable are your words,
For not even a shadow
Passes before my unfrequented dwelling.

Just like his letters, the prince arrived unannounced. Yet I, thinking he would not come at all, and tired with the religious observances of several days, had fallen asleep. No one noticed his gentle knocking at the gate. He, on the other hand, had heard some rumors, and suspecting the presence of another lover, quietly retired.

THE IZUMI SHIKIBU NIKKI

On the morning of the next day, a letter arrived:

> *I stood before your gate*
> *Never to be opened.*
> *There: your pitiless heart!*

I tasted the bitterness of love, and was bitterly sad.

Truly! I thought, *He has visited me last night! How careless of me to fall asleep.* And I wrote back:

> *How can you judge,*
> *A door so closely shut,*
> *The nature of my heart?*

It seems you entertain various strange suspicions—O that I could lay bare my heart to you!

The next night he wanted to come again, yet he was advised against it. He feared the criticism of the lord keeper of the privy seal[11] and the crown prince,[12] so his visits became more and more sporadic.

Summer Rains

The continuous early-summer rains of May had set in, and gazing at the unbroken clouds I worried and thought, *What is to come of our relationship? I have had many men make advances at me. Yet presently, though I think nothing of it, it seems people are spreading all kinds of strange rumors, and* "whenever someone disappears, whenever I appear, someone else is hurt, and so it might be better for me to also disappear."[13]

Then it was that a letter from Prince Atsumichi arrived, with the words:

How are you keeping during these dreary days of rain?

You may think it

THE IZUMI SHIKIBU NIKKI

The usual early summer rains of May
Yet in truth they are my tears
Shedded as I pine for you
Amid today's long spell of rain.

Reading the poem I realized how thoughtful it had been of the prince to write to me at this gloomy time of year and though, *He thought of me amid my reveries!*

So I replied:

Unaware of the sadness in your heart,
I knew only of the rain in mine.[14]

And turning the page over I wrote:

It passes,
The world's sorrowful life—
Let today's long rains
Wash me and my sorrows away.

Is there someone equal to equinoctial week to stop these rains and rescue me?

As soon as the prince had read my letter he sent a messenger back with his reply:

> *Helpless man,*
> *I am weary even of life.*
> *Not to you alone*
> *Beneath the sky*
> *Is rain and dulness.*

I too suffer from this weary world.

The Flooded River

It was the fifth day of May—the summer rain was still gently falling. The prince had been touched by my answer of the day before, which was deeper in feeling, and on that morning of heavy rain he wrote with much kindness to inquire after me:

> *Wasn't the sound of last evening's rain terrifying?*

I replied:
> *Of what was I thinking*
> *All the long night through*
> *Listening to the rain against the window?*[15]
> *What else but you?*

*I was sheltered, yet the sleeve that might have remained
dry had I gone out, now grows moist with tears inside.*[16]

Thus I wrote to the prince, and he thought, *Well, she is sensitive; words have an effect on her.* And he replied:

> *All the night through,*
> *It was of you I thought—*
> *How is it that you remain indoors,*
> *Safe from the rain outside,*
> *Without a man to guard you?*

At noon people said, "The Kamo River has burst its banks!" and many went to see it. The prince also went to see, and wrote:

How are you at present? I have just gone to see the flooding.

> *The rains have made the river burst its banks.*
> *Yet what is it compared to this heart of mine,*
> *Which overflows with feelings.*

THE IZUMI SHIKIBU NIKKI

Do you know this?

And I wrote:

> *No waters around me flow.*
> *No depth lies here*
> *To make you drown,*
> *Yet you fail to appear.*[17]

Poems alone are not enough.

The prince made up his mind to come, and ordered perfumery for himself. Just then his old wet nurse, Jiju no Menoto, came up, and said, "Where are you going? People are talking. That lady is not of high birth. If you wish her to serve you, you should summon her to the palace as a servant. Your undignified excursions are truly unseemly. Among those who visit her are a large number of men. Something untoward may happen. All this started with some man named Ukon no Jō. He accompanied the late prince too. If you wander out in the depth of night no good can come of it. I will tell the prime minister[18] of the persons who accompany you on these nightly escapades. The world is ever changing; no one can tell what will happen tomorrow. The late minister loved you much and asked the present one to look kindly on you. Yet you must keep yourself from these indiscretions till worldly affairs are more settled."

The prince said, "Then where shall I go? I am lonely, and am merely seeking to divert myself. People are foolish to make much of it."

Yet even as he spoke he thought, *Truly, though she may be uncannily indifferent, yet she is the one I had longed for. So why not bring her to the palace and keep her as my concubine?*

At the same time he reflected that if he did so yet more painful rumors might be spread, and in this troubled state of mind his visits to her grew less and less.

The Morning Rooster

At length, with great difficulty, Prince Atsumichi visited me.

"I could not come in spite of my desires," he said with great sincerity. "Please do not think that I neglect you. The fault is in you: I have heard that there are many friends of yours who are jealous of me, and I am merely staying away so as not to burden you with their slander. And then there is also my appearance in the eyes of society, which makes me even more reluctant to do so."

He continued: "Come with me for this night only. There is a hidden place no one knows, where the two of us can talk at leasure."

Then he ordered his carriage and made me get in against my wishes, so I reluctantly complied and went with him, frightfully anxious lest anyone might find out. Yet it was already growing late and no one around to see us.

At length the prince quietly drew up his carriage along a corridor without any sign of life and got out.

"Get off," he said forcibly, and I did as he instructed, though I felt tormented and thought it disgraceful to be so conspicuous in the bright moonlight.

Then he gently whispered, "Well, what do you think? Isn't it nice and secluded? Here we can from now on meet without anyone knowing about us. At your residence I am always anxious about other men. I can never be at ease there."

When dawn came he made me get into the carriage and said, "I should really go with you, but since it is broad daylight I fear people may think I have passed the night outside the court."

On my way home I thought, *What a strange rendezvous. What on earth will people think!*

Yet, at the same time, the uncommonly beautiful features of the prince at dawn lingered in my mind.

I wrote to him:

> *Rather would I urge*
> *Your early return at evening*
> *Than ever again*
> *Make you rise at dawn*
> *It is so sorrowful.*

He replied:

> *Compared to your departure*
> *In the morning dew*
> *It were better to come back*
> *Unsatisfied at night.*

Let us drive away such thoughts. I cannot visit you, as your residence lies in an unlucky direction tonight. I can only go out and meet you halfway.

I though *How unseemly. This cannot go on forever, with me visiting him all the time.* But like the previous evening, he appeared in his carriage and said, "Hurry, hurry!"

What a disgrace, I thought, yet I stole out into the carriage and we went to the same place where we had gone the previous evening and spent the night talking. His legal wife, the princess, was under the illusion that was spending the night at the residence of his father, Emperor Reisen.

At dawn he said:

The harsh cry of the morning rooster announces our sad parting.[19]

Then he joined me in my carriage and saw me home. On the way there he said, "Always come with me like this."

I replied, "How can it always be so?"

And having brought me home, he returned to the palace.

Before long another letter arrived. Attached to it was a rooster's feather:

This morning the rooster's cry was hateful to me and thus I killed it.

> *Though the harbinger*
> *Of our sad parting*

THE IZUMI SHIKIBU NIKKI

Now lies silent,
I still feel empty.
Yet I could not forgive
That ignorant cry.

I replied:

The sad call
Of the morning rooster
I know it well.
Announcing yet another morning
Spent without you.

The Hill of Pines

Two or three days had passed, the moon was wonderfully bright, and I was sitting on the edge of the veranda looking at the spectacle, when a letter from the prince arrived:

What are you doing at this moment? Are you gazing at the moon?

> *Are you, like me*
> *Thinking of the moon*
> *Over the mountain's edge?*
> *Melting together for eternity.*

His letter was more elegant than usual. And it consoled

me, for just then I had been thinking how bright the moon had been when we were together at the palace and fretting whether anyone might have seen us.

I answered:

> *Gazing at the moon*
> *I think of that night*
> *When it shone down on us,*
> *Yet my heart is empty*
> *And my eyes are vacant*
> *Without you.*

I mused alone until the day dawned. The next night the prince came again, but I was not aware of it. I was sharing my house with the rest of my family, and spotting a carriage intended for one of my sisters he thought, *A carriage! Another man is visiting her!*

Yet even though he was unhappy he was not ready yet to break off his ties with me and sent me another letter:

> *Did you know I visited you last night? It pains me even more to think you might not even have noticed.*

> *The hill of pines,*
> *Threatened by the crowding waves*
> *Today is washed away*
> *By your infidelity.*[20]

It was raining heavily when I received his letter, and I thought, *I don't understand! Someone must have told the prince a falsehood*, and I wrote:

> *You, and you alone*
> *Are my longed-for island.*
> *Is it not for someone else*
> *That you have swept me aside?*

Thus I replied, but the prince being troubled by the previous night, did not write to me for a long time.

Then, at last, there was word from the prince:

> *Love and misery*
> *In various shapes*
> *Pass through my mind*
> *Never to rest.*

I wanted to answer, but feared he might construe it as an excuse, so I merely wrote:

> *Let it be as you will,*
> *I will not pine,*
> *Wether you come or not,*
> *yet to part without bitter feeling*
> *Would have eased my sorrow.*

From that time onward we seemed to grow apart.

Silver Moon

One moon-bright night, I was lying near the veranda of my house, gazing at the moon and could not help thinking, *How I envy the moon's serene course amid this gloomy world.*[21] And I composed a poem for the prince:

> *In her deserted house*
> *She gazes at the moon*
> *He is not coming*
> *And she cannot reveal her heart*
> *There is none who will listen.*

I handed it to my toilet maid and told her, "Hand this to master Ukon no Jō."

Just then Prince Atsumichi was in the presence of the emperor, conversing with others. When the latter had left, and Ukon no Jō offered the letter to the prince, the prince said "Prepare my carriage—the inconspicuous one I always use." And at last he came to me again.

I was still languishing near the veranda, gazing at the moon, when I heard someone enter the house and, going to the rear of the house, lowered the *sudare*. And there he was, like always, except that this time he was not in his court robe, but in his everyday wear, which was more soft yet wonderfully splendid.

Then, without explaining himself further, he placed a written poem on his fan and passed it under the *sudare* saying, "Since your messenger returned without awaiting my answer, I have come to deliver it in person."

I felt awkward talking to him from such a distance, so I held out my own fan to receive his letter.

The prince now wanted to come in. And standing among the beautiful shrubs in the garden, he began to recite:

My beloved is like a dewdrop on a leaf...[22]

How elegant, how graceful the allusion was. Then he drew nearer and said, "I must now return. I came to ascertain it was I to whom you were alluding in your poem. Tomorrow is a day of fasting, and people will talk if I am not at the palace."

He was about to depart when I exclaimed, "Oh, that another shower might come! So that like the passing rays of moonlight, you might linger here for just another while!"

At this he realized I was more innocent and child-like than those around him asserted. "Ah, dear one," he said, and came inside for a while. Then he went away, saying:

> *Unwillingly urged*
> *By the moon on her clouded course*
> *My shadow must depart,*
> *But not my heart.*

When he was gone I had the *sudare* drawn up and read the poem he had presented to me on his fan:

> *She is gazing at the moon,*
> *But claims her thoughts are all of me*

THE IZUMI SHIKIBU NIKKI

Is it true? I wonder
And draw towards her side.

Well, I though, *he is, after all, a man of refinement! Though he might have been told I am just a worthless woman, somehow he seems to have changed his mind.*

He, on his side, seems to have though, *Lady Shikibu is not just anyone and needs consoling in her moments of loneliness.* Yet those who served him said, "It seems Minamoto Masamichi, too, is visiting her, and even stays with her in daytime." Others still said, "Minamoto Toshikata also visits her." And so mouths kept wagging and kept the prince from writing to me.

A Sailor's Vessel

One day his highness's young page, who was fond of my toilet maid, came to the house. While they were chattering she asked him, "Is there a letter from Prince Atsumichi?" To this he answered, "No. The other night my lord came to visit your lady, but found a palanquin at the gate. From that time he does not write letters. It seems he has heard that other men visit this place."

When she told me what he had said I though, *For a long while now, I have asked for neither this nor that, as I did not want to impose myself upon the prince. And only at those moment when he cared to think of me did I hope we might be together. Yet of all things I now have to be the object of suspicion because of this rediculous rumor!*

THE IZUMI SHIKIBU NIKKI

I felt crushed in body and spirit and lamented, *Why fret in this manner when life is so short,*[23] when a letter was brought to me:

> *I am strangely ill and much troubled these days. Of late I visited you, but you were already seeing someone else and I returned. I feel you are treating me like a child.*
>
> > *Let it be*
> > *I will let my sorrows sail*
> > *As you are leaving me*
> > *Like a sailor's little vessel*
> > *Parting from its rocky shore.*

Though it pained me to reply, lest it might be construed as an excuse for the outrageous slander he had heard, I though, *Just this once*, and wrote:

> > *Off the shore of aimlessness*
> > *With burning heart and dripping sleeves,*
> > *I am cast adrift*
> > *In a sailor's little vessel.*

Tanabata

While Prince Atsumichi and I were thus exchanging letters, July had arrived. On Tanabata,[24] the evening of the seventh day, I received many love letters from amorous men writing, "You are my Alpha. I am your Altair. Let us meet tonight." Yet they did not catch my fancy. *Can it be*, I thought, *that the price, who has never missed an opportunity in the past to write me a letter at such an elegant occasion—can it be that he has now forgotten all about me?*

At last there came a poem, but all he wrote was:

> *Alas! that I should become the one*
> *Who can only gaze at the weaving one*
> *Beyond the river of heaven.*

Despite the irony of it all, I saw that he could not forget me and was pleased:

> *How can I look towards the heavens,*
> *Even a heaven watched by you,*
> *On this Weaver's Festival*
> *When I do not star in you firmament?*

This I wrote, in the hope that as he read, he would feel that he must not desert me.

Towards the end of the month he wrote to me:

I fear we are growing more and more apart. Why do you not write to me occasionally? It seems I cannot get you to think of me, if only as a friend.

I replied:

> *Because you do not wake you cannot hear*
> *The autumn wind, sighing in the silver reeds*
> *Keeping me awake, pining for you*
> *Ah, nights and nights of autumn!*

No sooner had the prince received my letter, than he wrote to me:

O my beloved, how can you believe my sleep to be untroubled? Lately sad thoughts have been mine and sleep is never sound.

Like the wind stirs into life
The common reeds
That grow at Naniwa
I will not sleep,
But listen
How it's sigh
Stirs whole my heart.[25]

Autumn

After two days, Prince Atsumichi unexpectedly came to me at dusk and drew up his palanquin into the courtyard. As it was still light, and he had never before made his appearance at this time of day, I was terribly embarrassed. Yet it could not be helped, so I let him in. And after some superficial conversation he left again.

Several day passed without any letters from him, and growing increasingly anxious, I at last wrote:

> *Wearily the autumn days drag by*
> *With no word from you*
> *Boding silence!*

Now I understand the words, 'Always I yearn for you, yet how strange the yearning of an autumn evening!'[26] Be that as it may, last night you acted strangely. Could it be that you were on your way to see someone else?

He replied:

As of late I have been detained at the palace, however,

> *Though days pass*
> *And others may forget*
> *I can never lose the thought*
> *Of that evening's meeting*
> *On an autumn day.*

And thus, though we sought to console each other with the exchange of incoherent and meaningless poems, when I came to think of it, I felt more wretched than ever.

Ishiyama

Thus the days passed, and when August came I though, *Why not go to the Ishiyama temple[27] to revive my doleful spirit, and stay there for a week or so?*

It was around that time that Prince Atsumichi thought, *It has been a while since I met Lady Shikibu*, and said to his page: "Here is a letter for Lady Shikibu."

The page replied: "I went to her house the other day and heard that she has lately gone to the Ishiyama temple."

"Then it is already late in the day—tomorrow morning you shall go," and he sat down and wrote a letter.

The next morning, the page arrived at the Ishiyama temple with the letter. I was so homesick for the capital that I was not sitting in front of the Buddha, but near the temple's veranda, praying with all my heart, when I spotted someone below the balustrade and saw it was the page.

Though I was happy, I was surprised to see a familiar face at such an unexpected place and sent over my maid to ask him what brought him here.

She came back with the prince's letter and I opened it with more haste than usual:

> *You seem to be very devout in your religious pursuits. Why is it that you did not even care to tell me of this? I cannot imagine that you consider me a hindrance to your devotion to Buddha. Yet it pains me to think that you left me behind in this manner.*
>
> > *Do you feel*
> > *How my soul wanders after you,*
> > *Crossing the Ausaka barrier?*[28]
> > *O ceaseless longing!*
>
> *When shall you return from the mountains?*

Though he had not taken the trouble to send me word

when I was near, I was nevertheless delighted he had gone through all the trouble of sending a messenger to this remote place, and answered:

> *While I was away*
> *It seemed you had forgotten*
> *A way to meet me,*
> *Yet who is this*
> *Coming across the barrier?*

You ask when I will leave the mountain—do you think I have come here on a whim?

> *While on Mount Nagara*
> *My yearning is towards*
> *The open water of Lake Biwa;*
> *The beach of departure*
> *Does not lie towards*
> *The Royal City.*

Reading my poem the prince said to his page, "I am sorry to trouble you, but please go to Ishiyama once more."

He wrote:

In your letter you wondered who had come to see you:

> *What use is it to send my page*
> *Across the barrier of meeting*
> *If you pretend not to know me?*[29]

Can this be true?

> *Even if your pilgrimage is done on a whim,*
> *Cast at least your eyes on Uchide*[30]
> *On the shores of Lake Biwa!*

I replied merely with a poem:

> *The tears I would shed*
> *At the though of meeting you*
> *At the Ausaka barrier*
> *Would suffice to fill Lake Biwa.*

And in the margin I wrote:

> *I have come to Ishiyama*
> *To strengthen my resolve,*
> *So come and tempt me*
> *Back towards the capital.*

Reading this the prince realized he wanted to meet me at the most unexpected of moments, yet how could he, given his social standing?

Following this exchange of letters I left the mountains and returned to the capital. Upon my return I received a letter from the prince:

> *You wrote "come and tempt me back towards the capital," yet I see that you have already returned from the Ishiyama temple, so I cannot now go out and meet you:*
>
> > *I am taken aback!*
> > *Who can it be*
> > *Who tempted you*
> > *From straying from the Buddhist path*
> > *And return to the capital?*

All I could do was reply with another poem:

> *Out of the mountains*
> *Leaving the path of light*
> *I wrap myself in darkness,*
> *Solely for your sake.*

Towards the end of August, a devastating wind blew hard, and autumn rains lashed the roofs. I was immerged in thought and even sadder than usual, when a letter was brought from the prince.

I reflected on how the prince had never missed an occasion in keeping with the season to inquire after me, so I did feel inclined to forgive him his usual heartless trespasses.

His letter read:

> *In sorrow I gaze*
> *Upon the sky of autumn*
> *The clouds are in turmoil*
> *And the wind blows hard.*

And I answered:

THE IZUMI SHIKIBU NIKKI

The wind of autumn
Even if it gently blows
Makes me sad
How the more sad am I
On this clouded stormy day!

It seemed the prince understood how I felt, yet as usual, another month passed by without him visiting me.

Daybreak

It was the dawn of the twentieth day of September, and the morning moon hung in the western sky. The prince awoke and thought to himself, *It has been a while since I last saw Lady Shikibu. She will surely be looking at the moon. Will there be someone with her watching it?* Then he went over to my place, accompanied just by his faithful page, and knocked at the gate.

It so happened that I was lying awake, thinking about this and that, and feeling quite forlorn and melancholic, perhaps the more so because of the season. *How strange!* I though. *Who can it be at this early hour?* And so I woke my maid and told her to inquire who it was that called. But she took ages to get up, and when she finally did she stumbled around in her confusion, by which time the knocking at the gate had stopped. *Have they left?* I wondered. *Surely, they will have thought I am a deep sleeper, which will give them the impression I have no troubles. Might it have been someone like me, unable to sleep? Oh, who could it have been?*

At length my manservant, having been roused by the maid, returned and said, *There is no one at the gate. You must have just imagined it. How typical of a lady of the manor to get all flustered at this time of night and make a scene!* And having vented his spleen he went back to bed.

Needless to say I could not close my eyes after that and spent the rest of the night gazing at the morning fog, hanging heavily in the air. It turned light and I began to put to paper the things I had on my mind, when I unexpectedly received a latter from the prince with just a poem:

> *In the autumn night*
> *The pale morning moon was setting*
> *When I turned away from the closed door.*

Oh my, I thought, *how disappointed he must have been.* At the same time I thought, *Still, he hasn't failed to think of me with the changing of season*, for *he cannot have failed to notice that serenely beautiful sky*. And so, without making any changes, I folded my rambling jottings into a knotted letter and sent them to him.

Jottings

The prince received my knotted letter and read:

The wind blows hard as if determined to blow away the last leaves on the branch, and I am more sad than ever. It grows cloudy and threatening, the rain is drizzling down softly, and I am hopelessly desolate.

> *Before the autumn ends*
> *My sleeves will become moldy with tears.*
> *On whose sleeve can I shed my tears*
> *Come early winter?*

I am wretched, yet who will understand? Even the reeds

have now lost their color. And though winter has not yet arrived, already the reeds are cruelly beaten down before the storms that will carry the early winter rains. And I grow afraid, fearful that I too will be swept away like the lingering dew. And so I linger, like the withered leaves, unable to go inside, but lie near the veranda, unable to sleep. All those around me are sound asleep, while I lie here, eyes wide open, unable to decide on this or that, consumed by my misery, when the faint call of geese stirs in me the saddest of thoughts:

> *Unable even to daze,*
> *Aah, how many nights*
> *Have passed*
> *With the sole call*
> *Of wild geese.*

Why spend the night just listening to the call of geese? *I thought, and threw open the shutters, when I saw the moon declining in the west, distant yet serenely transparent. The morning dew hovered above the earth, and the sound of the morning bell merged with the call of*

THE IZUMI SHIKIBU NIKKI

a rooster. And it felt that all the days that had passed and all that lay ahead came together to make me feel as I had never done before, and that even the tears that stained my sleave were fresher than ever:

> *Someone, besides just me*
> *Will be gazing at the pale morning moon,*
> *Feeling like I do.*
> *What is more sorrowful*
> *Than a September dawn?*

How would I feel if, just now, someone came knocking at my gate? Truly, is there anyone who spends the night like me, lying awake and gazing at the moon?

> *There must be one of like mind to me*
> *Musing on the morning moon.*
> *But how to find him out!*

I had received the prince's letter just when I was finishing this very letter, and so I had sent it as it was, knotted, without any further changes.

And though the prince read my letter and did not think anything strange about it, it did not prompt him to come and visit me. But realizing I was in this frame of mind, he immediately dispatched a letter of his own.

I was still languishing near the veranda of my house, looking outside, when the prince's page delivered his letter, and I anxiously opened it:

Autumn is here.
And though you think
It is just your sleeves
That grow moldy with tears
Mine too have grown moldy.

Do not think yourself
The vanishing dew.
Think instead
Of the long-blooming
Chrysanthemum flower.

It is not the melancholy cry
Of geese above the clouds,

HEAN COURT HEROINES

*But the call of your heart
To which your ears are tuned.*

*There is another
With thoughts like mine,
Who is gazing toward the sky
Of the morning moon.*

*To you I went
Believing only you
Were gazing at the moon like me,
Even though we were apart.
Yet here I am this morning,
Having returned home
not knowing
You were awake.*

O, why was that gate so hard to open!

So my jottings had not been in vain after all!

Ghost Writer

Towards the end of September I had another letter from Prince Atsumichi. Starting out by excusing himself for his late neglect he wrote:

> *I have an awkward thing to ask you. There is a lady with whom I have been secretly intimate. She is going away to a distant province and I want to send her a poem that will touch her heart deeply. Everything you write touches me, so please compose a poem for me.*

What impudence! I thought. *To brag about a thing like that!* I though of telling him I could not be his ghost writer, but this seemed a bit too cheeky, so instead I wrote:

How can you ask me to write a poem like that?

> *In the tears of regret*
> *Your image will linger long*
> *Even after chilly autumn has gone.*
> *It is painful for me to write*
> *A heartfelt letter in your stead.*

And in the margin I wrote:

> *Where can it be*
> *That she must go*
> *And leave you behind?*
> *Even while I am able*
> *To share with you*
> *This painful union?*

The prince wrote back:

Though I could write that your first poem is excellent, I would reproach myself for pretending to be a good judge of poems. Yet I must say your second poem is irksome to me. You write of our "painful union," but I have to say that I do not see it in that light:

> *I could not care less*
> *About the one who must go*
> *And leave me behind.*
> *As long as I am in the thoughts*
> *Of the one who is without equal.*

As long as this is true, I can go on living in this cruel world.

Pillow Talk

It was October and on the tenth day the prince came to see me. As it was now dark inside the house, we sat near the veranda and spent the time in the tenderest of pillow talk. It was drizzling down with rain and every now and then the moon peaked from among the coulds. It felt as if this moment had been created just for the two of us, and shivers ran down my spine with the excitement of it all.

Observing me in this state, the prince must have though to himself, *It's strange how people say she is fickle and scandalous—isn't she innocent and lovable?*

He was overcome by pity and roused me from my feigned slumber—in truth my heart was in a state of delightful bewilderment—and said,

THE IZUMI SHIKIBU NIKKI

It is not dripping rain
Nor morning dew,
Yet strangely wet
Is my arm's pillow
On which you rest
Your weary head.

I was overwhelmed by emotion and could not speak, but he saw my tears glistening in the moonlight.

He was touched and said, "Why do you not speak? Have my idle words displeased you?"

I replied: "I do not know why, for though I have taken your words to heart, it is in a state of utter confusion. I suppose you will just have to wait and see," I said softly, "whether I will forget your arm's pillow.'"

And thus, as we exchanged our playful repartees, the night passed and dawn broke.

The prince returned to the palace, and realizing I had no other man I could rely on he wrote,

How are you faring now?

I answered:

> *Have they dried?*
> *Those sleeves of yours?*
> *Slightly moist with tears,*
> *Of a dreamlike moment*
> *On your arm's pillow.*

He read it and smiled—I had not forgotten his "arm's pillow," and he thought it tasteful.

He replied:

> *You say it was only in a dream*
> *That my sleeves were wet with tears:*
> *Yet here I am, unable to sleep,*
> *My sleeves drenched with your tears.*

What to Do?

Perhaps it was the charm of the mid-October air that deeply touched his heart and jolted his feelings towards me, but after our last meeting Prince Atsumichi took pity on me and frequently visited me. And the more he saw of me, the more he realized I was not at all used to men around me, but merely helpless and forlorn, which made him pity me all the more.

While he was earnestly explaining all this to me he said, "You are always this pensive aren't you? It is not that I have thought this through yet, but right now I just want you to come and live with me. It seems that those around me criticize my conduct as unbecoming. Maybe it is that I don't visit you enough. And while I haven't seen amy other men

HEIAN COURT HEROINES

around here, still, apart from those around me spawning the most hateful of rumors, the numberless times I have visited you in vain have left me disconsolate, making me feel as if I'm not taken seriously and often causing me to wonder, *What on earth shall I do?*"

"Maybe it's just me being old-fashioned, but I simply dread the though of losing you. Still, I simply cannot go on visiting you in this manner. Soon people will hear of my true conduct. Untill then, since I cannot say when we will meet again:

> *Do not forget me.*
> *Though we may be*
> *As far apart as earth and heaven,*
> *Remember me until I return,*
> *Like the moon*
> *On its celestial journey.*[31]

However, if you really feel as loneliness as you say, why not come with me to the palace? It is true than my wife, as well as others, reside there. Yet this need not be a problem. Perhaps it is because such escapades do not suit me, but there are no women consorting with me when no one is around, and even when I am at my religious devotions I am all on my own. Would it not be a great consolation, I think to myself, to have a kindred soul like you around to talk to and share my feelings with?"

I thought, *How could I, after all this time, ever get used to a life like that? Indeed, I likewise was asked and likewise refused to tend on the prince's brother, Prince Morosada. If only I had, as the poem goes, 'a dwelling among the Yoshino Mountains where I could flee from this vale of tears!'[32] Yet who is there to guide me to such a refuge? I feel as if my life is 'one long night from which there is no dawn to brighten my days, spent at some forlorn place where the* hototogisu *sings all to itself.'[33] It is true that there have been many men who sought to court me with trivial pleasantries, yet now the world seems to think I am a base woman. In the end there is only Prince Atsumichi on whom I can truly rely. Perhaps I should do as the prince asks. It is true his legal wife resides at the palace, but they do not share the same quarters, and those who attend on the prince are all wet nurses. Of course, I must avoid going in front of other people and trumpet our affair to the world, yet as long as I will be staying in a secluded part of the palace, what can go wrong? No matter how one looks at it, at leas those false accusation of me seeing other men will be laid to rest once and for all.*

And so I said, "It isn't that, like the monk Gyōson, I think, 'Cherry blossom! Have pity on me! No one else truly understands me.'[34] But I do feel that the only time I find relief from such feelings is when I wait for you and talk with you, even though it isn't often. And while I really want to do as you say, people are already saying it is unbecoming of you to visit me, even though we are living far apart. How much more, then, will they be inclined to say, 'The rumors are true!' if I were to move to the palace."

The prince said, "It will be to me that they will say this or that, not you, at any rate. I will find you an inconspicuous place and let you know in due time."

And thus, having given me much hope, he returned before dawn.

I remained behind and just lay there, languishing near the veranda with the latticed gate still open, thinking to myself thought like, *What shall I do?* and *Won't people laugh?* when there was a letter from the prince:

> *Dawn broke*
> *As I walked along the morning path.*
> *Sodden my arm-pillow sleeves*
> *With morning dew,*
> *With parting tears.*

Again he had referred to his "arm pillow." And though it was a bit of a commonplace, he had not forgotten about our little exchange, and I was pleased:

> *Your sleeves are wet*
> *With the dew of grass*
> *Along the morning path.*
> *And so are mine,*
> *Yet not with dew.*

Head Start

The next night the moon was very bright. Both the prince at the palace and I at home had spent the night gazing at the moon. The prince, intending to write me a letter as usual, asked, "Is my page in attendance?"

Meanwhile I on my side, surprised by the whiteness of the morning's hoar frost, sent a poem to the prince:

> *There was frost*
> *On the sleeves of my arm pillow,*
> *Waking this morning,*
> *I found it totally white!*

The prince was sorry I had got a head start on him, so he

sat down to write me the following poem:

> *It is my waking thoughts*
> *Pining for you*
> *Deposited as early morning frost.*

Just then the page finally presented himself and the prince said, "Where have you been?" His assistant took the page aside and handed him the letter saying, "You're late! His majesty is very upset with you!"

The page hurried over and presented the letter to me, saying, "His Highness had called me, but then your message arrived, and now he is mad with me."

I opened the letter and read its content:

Wasn't last night's moon beautiful?

> *All night I was awake,*
> *Gazing at the moon*
> *While you soundly slept,*
> *Yet there was none*
> *To bear these tidings to you.*

THE IZUMI SHIKIBU NIKKI

I thought, *So the page is right: the prince did intend to send me a letter before I did!* I was delighted:

> *I did not close an eye,*
> *Gazing at the moon all night.*
> *Is it true that you were gazing too,*
> *Waking until the frosted dawn?*

Then I thought it was funny he should have scolded the page, and in the margin I wrote:

> *Like the warm rays*
> *Of the rising sun*
> *dispels this morning's frost,*
> *So may your heart*
> *Melt toward this hapless page.*

I think the page is really disheartened...

His answer soon followed:

I think it quite odious that you should be so pleased with yourself for getting a head start on me this morning. In truth I have a mind of killing the chap for being the cause of it all in the first place!

> *The early rays*
> *May melt the morning frost,*
> *Yet it does not seem to lift*
> *Nor does my mood.*

I thought, *What a thing to say—to 'have a mind of killing the chap,'* and replied:

You hardly show your face yourself, yet here you are, thinking of taking the 'life' of the very same page—my sole consolation—whom you casually send on his way with the words, 'lively now!'

At this the prince had to laugh and replied:

> *How right you are*
> *My hidden wife:*
> *How cauld I hurt him now?*

Yet all we do is talk about this page; have you perhaps forgotten the sweet memory of my arm's pillow?

At this I wrote:

> *How can you even think*
> *I could forget that night*
> *My head on your arm's pillow.*
> *I, who have waged my heart*
> *On my love for you?*

But he replied:

> *Would you have remembered?*
> *Had I not mentioned,*
> *My arm's pillow?*

Moongazing

Two or three days passed without any word from the prince, and I wondered, *Whatever happened to his promise to bring me to the palace?* This thought kept me busy all day, so that, when night came, I could not sleep, but just lay there, awake, my eyes wide open. It was already growing late, when I heard someone knocking at the gate. I could not think who it might be, but when my servant went out to ask, it was a messenger with a letter from the price.

Surprised to receive a letter at this late hour, I was also delighted at the idea that I had made the prince understand and kept him awake and write a poem for me, which made me think of the lines, "Lying awake each and every night with the thought of you, my heart flies towards you to awaken your heart."[35] And so I threw open the wooden shutters and read the prince's letter in the moonlight:

> *Are you gazing*
> *At this late hour,*
> *At the autumn moon*
> *Serenely bright*
> *Over the ridge*
> *Of yonder mountain?*

I gazed at the moon and let his words play on my lips as I though of him more tenderly than ever before.

I had accepted the letter without opening the front gate, and thought of the messenger, eagerly waiting outside, so I quickly wrote down my answer:

> *Though it is late*
> *I cannot sleep.*
> *Yet to look at the moon*
> *Is only to miss you more.*
> *So I refrain from looking.*

The prince, who had expected me to be gazing at the moon like him, was taken aback and though, *Clearly, this isn't someone whom I can pass over. Somehow I want to have her close to me so that we can freely exchange such refined thoughts.*

Spindle Tree

After two days the prince visited me secretly in a women's carriage. He had never before seen me in broad daylight, and I felt awkward.[36] Still, our's wasn't the kind of relationship where I could shyly withdraw because I felt it might be unsightly. I also thought to myself, *If he is truthful in his offer to bring me to the palace, I cannot go on being shy and withdrawn like this forever.* And so I inched forward into the sunlight to welcome him.

The prince warmly excused himself for his recent silence, and having laid down and held me briefly, he said, "As I said before, do make up your mind. I just cannot get used to these outings, though I dread not seeing you and find our uncertain relationship more than excruciating."

I said, "I want to do as you say, whatever it may be, but does not the poem go, 'When at first the lovers meet, the more they do, the more they want to see each other; yet the closer they grow, the more they tire of each other.'[37] Likewise, I fear that if I were to join you at the palace, you might tire of me."

"Very well then," he said as he left the room, "come and find out for yourself. Just remember there is another poem that goes, 'Like the plain dress of Ise's salt dryers, lovers' love grows keener with the wearing.'[38]

There was a beautiful spindle tree among the hedge in front of my room, and its leaves were just turning red.[39] The prince bent over towards it and leaning against the balustrade he said:

> *Like the spindle tree's leaves*
> *Have gained in color,*
> *So our words of love*
> *Have gained in depth.*

And, taking up his poem, I continued:

The touch of dew
Deepens their hue,
To be carried away on the wind
Like our fleeting words.

Observing me, the prince was touched by the affectionate and refined aspect of the scene. And he, too, looked exceedingly splendid. For though he was attired in his regular court dress, I could just from below spot his inexplicably beautiful undergarment, which made him more desirable to me than ever in all his manly glory.

The Bridge

the next day I had a letter from the prince saying:

> *Yesterday I was sorry that you were embarrassed, yet to me you were lovable and utterly captivating.*

I replied:

> *The goddess of Mount Katsuragi*
> *Would have felt the same*
> *When she failed*
> *To bridge the divide at Kume.*[40]

What was I to do? I felt so awkward!

THE IZUMI SHIKIBU NIKKI

No sooner had I dispatched the letter than a messenger came back with his reply:

> *Had I the power*
> *Of En no Gyōja[40]*
> *I would dispel forthwith*
> *Your every doubt.*

After that he came oftener, which relieved my sadness more than ever.

Meanwhile evil men kept sending me amorous letters—they even visited my place and loitered about at the gate, causing rumors about me to fly again. I thought, *Perhaps I should indeed go to the palace*, but as before, I lost nerve and could not reach a clear decision one way or the other.

Autumn Colors

One early morning, when white frost covered the land, I wrote to the prince:

> *The plover cannot tell*
> *The tale of my frosted sleeve.*
> *Yet I wonder*
> *About the wing-like sleeves*
> *Of you, my phoenix?*

He replied:

> *How can there be tears*
> *On the sleeves of she*

THE IZUMI SHIKIBU NIKKI

Who is sleeping soundly.
Unlike the phoenix
Who wakes at night.

That same evening, he came to see me, and the next morning he said, "The maple trees up in the mountains are changing color. Come, let us go and watch the spectacle together!"

I replied, "That sounds delightful." Yet when the appointed day came, I excused myself, saying I had to fast, and stayed inside.

"That is disappointing," said the prince. "Please don't miss this time of year, lest the leaves will have fallen."

But that night there blew an autumn gale that sounded so fierce that I could not imagine a leaf had been left hanging. I woke up and cited, "Were I a leaf in the raging storm, what cares would I have, but fall without regret?"[41] And so I spent the night, thinking to myself, *Surely all the leaves will have fallen by now; what a shame I didn't go and watch them with the prince.*

Early next morning, there was a letter from the prince:

*This inevitable rain
Of the tenth month,
The month of the absent gods,*[42]
*May be just another spell to you.
Though it is nothing less
Than the outpour of my tears.*

How sad that the leaves have fallen.

I wrote:

*Is it a mere autumn shower?
Is it my sodden sleeves?
I am at a loss to say.*

Then I added:

Truly, it is as you say—

*Last night's rain
Has washed away
The turning leaves.*

THE IZUMI SHIKIBU NIKKI

*If only I had gone
With you among the mountains
To watch them fall,
Before it was too late.*

The prince replied:

*How right you are:
If only you had joined me!
Yet why lament
At this new dawn
What cannot be undone?*

And in the margin there was another poem:

*Though I believe
No maple leaves are hanging
On the boughs,
Yet we may go and see
If scattering ones remain.*

I replied:

> *If only the evergreen*
> *Of the eternal mountains*
> *Showed one red leaf,*
> *I would join you*
> *To go and see it.*

Is it not folly to go at this late stage?

The other day, when the prince visited me, he had recalled how I had excused myself, saying I was inconvenienced and could not meet him. I had replied by saying:

> *Make haste, make haste*
> *Come to me in your flatboat.*
> *For I have brushed aside*
> *The common weed that kept you.*

But he replied:

Have you forgotten?

> *In a carriage we had planned to go*

THE IZUMI SHIKIBU NIKKI

To watch the turning of the leaves.
So how can I now
Come to meet you in a boat?

To which I rejoined:

How can I be charmed
By the turning of the leaves
If I have to linger here.
So come and hurry to me
Lest I too may fall.

Unlucky Directions

Night came and the prince visited me again. He said my dwelling was in an unlucky direction,[43] and that he had come to take me away.

At this time Prince Atsumichi was staying at the residence of his cousin, the Lieutenant General of the Third Rank, Fujiwara Kanetaka, equally so as to avoid having to travel in an inauspicious direction. I told him I thought it was terribly embarrassing, as I was already going to move to a place I didn't know in the first place. Yet he made me mount the carriage anyway, and when we arrived at the palace, he drew it into the empty oxcart shed and went inside, leaving me behind on my own in the carriage—I was petrified.

Finally, when all inside were fast asleep, he came to me and, getting inside the carriage, he sat with me, giving me all kind of assurances about our future together. Meanwhile night guards had come out and were patrolling the area, unaware of what was going on, while Ukon no Jō and his page were also in attendance.

He might find me lovable and express his fondness of me—he might profess to regret his hitherto wayward ways, yet in his conduct he remained utterly self-centered.

When dawn broke, he hastened to take me home. Then he hurried away to his cousin's residence, well in time before those inside had woken from their slumber.

In leaving he gave me a parting poem:

> *Though I should spend my night*
> *Sharing my bed and dreams with you,*
> *Here I am, awake at this early hour*
> *Inured to a life of sleepless nights.*

I replied:

> *Ever since that night*

When we shared our bed together,
I have been in the dark,
Clueless of my fate.
Yet here I was,
Spending the night alone
In some forsaken carriage,
Far away from home.

Yet how can I, I though to myself afterwards, *stay aloof and act as if nothing has happened, if he loves me, an unworthy woman, with such passion? Everything else is trivial.* And I decided, *I will go to the palace!*

Of course there were those who earnestly entreated me no to go and live with the prince, but I refused to listen. *Living like this is too painful anyhow*, I thought, *so why not trust my fate to providence? Still, I don't want to end up having to serve at court just because I live there. It truly is a situation of, 'What cavern will grant me the refuge from the world's ugly rumors.'[44] I would rather take the tonsure and live at a place where I cannot hear those detestable rumors. Yet what if I would encounter yet more hardships at such a place? Won't people think and say I did not do it for pure reasons? Isn't it better to stay in this world? After all, I do want to look after my parents and siblings, and secure the future of my daughter, Koshikibu no Naishi, my one memento of my late husband, Tachibana Michisada.*[45] *By joining the prince at the palace, I will at least put a stop to those troublesome rumors. And even if some rumor were to spread, if I am in close attendance on the prince, those around him will surely fathom the extent of the truth.*

And thus, having made up my mind, I refrained from responding altogether to any other suitors, and instructed my maids to tell those who might come to bring me letters that "Her ladyship is not at home!"

Rumors

There was a letter from the prince. He wrote:

> *I was a fool to believe you, to think there were no other men in your life.*

Apart from these words, there was just an old poem:

> *What you might think I do not know.*
> *I on my part hate to be talked about,*
> *So in present and in past*
> *I will pretend not to know you.*[46]

My heart was broken. Though there had hitherto been

many false rumors unworthy of attention, I had always let it pass, thinking, *Rumors may fly, yet how can I prove they are untrue?* But now the prince really seemed to believe them. I reflected, *There might be some who have heard I had made up my mind to join the prince at the palace, but how stupid will I end up looking if he drops me like this?* All this made me so miserable that I couldn't bring myself to answer his letter.

At the same time, while I agonized on what particular rumor had reached the prince's ear and thus refrained from replying, the prince, on his side, though, *She seems to be embarrassed by my earlier letter*, and wrote:

> *Why don't you reply to my letter? Am I to suppose the rumors are true then? You truly must be quick to change your heart. I had heard what they say about you, and though I had been taken aback, I had only reacted the way I did, thinking,*
>
> > *Rumors grow rampant,*
> > *Like the seaweed cut by fishers.*
> > *Yet they cannot touch me,*
> > *As long as I have your love.*[47]

This lifted my mood a little, and I wanted to know how he felt—what rumor might have come to his ear:

If you truly think of me,

> *Come to me, now!*
> *However much I want to show you,*
> *Want to meet you,*
> *Rumors will keep me,*
> *From joining you at the palace.*

The prince wrote back:

> *I now understand*
> *That you are afraid of rumors,*
> *But only when you're with me*
> *Not with other men.*

Rumors may spread, so does my anger.

I thought, *He is mocking me for not wanting to come and join him at the palace*. I though it cruel and replied:

Either way, this is terribly painful to me. I just wish you would understand how I feel!

He replied:

*I tell myself not to doubt,
Not to feel bitter,
Yet my heart will not follow.*

I answered:

*Let not your doubt of me
Fade from your heart.
For it is that same heart
That fervently believes in me.*

By now, it had already grown late, but that evening the prince came to me again. And he told me, "People are still talking about you, and I was so taken aback that I wrote the words I did. So if you don't want to hear such words, come and live with me." And having stayed the night, he returned to the palace.

In this manner, the prince kept sending me letters but seldom visited me.

One day, when the rain pelted down and the wind blew hard, the prince once again stayed away, and thinking, *He seems not to care about me, here at my windswept dwelling, with few to keep me company and few who visit me*, I wrote:

> *Everything is nipped by frost,*
> *And the autumn wind*
> *Stirs the silvergrass.*

The prince answered:

I feel for you when I hear these ominous winds blowing and think of how they might sound to you.

> *Everything fades and withers.*
> *How cruel the wind must sound,*
> *To you, in your solitary house,*
> *Visited by none but me.*

It pains me that I cannot visit you now.

Having read his letter, I though it strange that he had mentioned him being the only one to visit me.

Bliss

The prince sent his palanquin as usual, saying that he was at our hidden rendezvous, as his dwelling lay in an unlucky direction. By this stage I thought, *I had better do as he asks*, and went to meet him there.

The prince was in a gentle mood and we talked throughout the day and night, which helped to distract me from my feelings of loneliness and made me want to join him at the palace.

When the period of fasting had ended and I returned to my own dwelling, I felt more reluctant than ever to part with him, and overcome with longing I wrote:

In this hour of longing

THE IZUMI SHIKIBU NIKKI

Reflection brings to mind
Each day gone by
And in each one
Was less sorrow.

Reading my letter the prince, too, was overcome by longing and replied:

It is the same with me—

Is there a way
To make the bliss
Of yesterday
And the day before
The bliss of now?

Yet it is not sufficient to think it; so please make up your mind and join me here at the palace.

Still, I felt terribly daunted by the prospect and spent the rest of the day lost in idle reveries.

A Cold

By now the leaves of autumn had all fallen and though the sky was clear and bright, the last rays of the submerging sun looked so forlorn that I sent him a letter, as I had on so many evenings before:

> *My constant consolation you are,*
> *Yet with the end of day*
> *Sadness haunts me still.*

He replied:

> *All are sad*
> *When day draws to a close,*

THE IZUMI SHIKIBU NIKKI

Yet no one is sadder than you—
You, who speak of it
Before all others.

I feel for you when I think of it, and would love to come and visit you…

The next morning it was still early and frost lay white on the meadows, when the prince sent me a letter, inquiring:

How are you feeling now?

I replied with the words:

All night I lay awake,
Waiting for you.
And now,
With all the world
Wrapped in frost,
I feel more forlorn than ever.

As always the prince replied with many soft words:

Not having seen you,
I spent the night alone,
Pining for you.
I want for you to pine for me
The way I pine for you.

I answered:

To me there is no
"You are you" or "I am I."
How can two hearts
Not be as one
No—surely they are one!

By now I had caught a cold. And though it wasn't too bad, I was considerably inconvenienced, though the prince occasionally paid me a visit.

When I had recovered, the prince inquired:

How are you feeling now?

And I replied:

THE IZUMI SHIKIBU NIKKI

I am feeling a little better, and I am ashamed to say that I would like to live a little longer by your side. Still,

> *With your every receding step,*
> *So my life*
> *Seemed to recede from me.*
> *Yet your visits*
> *Brought me back to life.*

He wrote back:

I am so happy to hear you have recovered—

> *Your life's thread*
> *Cannot easily be broken,*
> *For it is tied together,*
> *With pledges of*
> *Long-enduring affection.*

And thus, as we exchanged messages, the year drew to a close, and I resolved to join the prince at the palace come spring.

Chinese Poems

November had come and it was snowing thick and fast, when the prince wrote to me:

> *Since the age of gods*
> *It has snowed,*
> *It is a known thing,*
> *Yet how fresh it seems*
> *This morning!*

I replied:

> *First snow!*
> *It is young with every winter,*

THE IZUMI SHIKIBU NIKKI

> *Yet I grow old*
> *As winter comes.*

Days were passed in exchanging these fancies. Then there was another letter from the prince:

It has been a while since I saw you, and just now I wanted to visit you, but now the people here have gathered to compose Chinese poems, so I cannot leave.

I wrote:

> *Had you no time to come?*
> *Then I would go to you.*
> *O that I knew an even way of love.*
> *(the art of composing poems).*

The prince was intrigued by my poem and replied.

Come to my mansion, and I will teach you the art of writing Chinese poems and art of finding me. But before all else, let us be together!

Frost

One early morning, when the frost lay brightly white upon the land, the prince wrote to me, saying:

What do you think of this morning's frost…

I replied:

> *Many a hundred times*
> *This morning's sandpiper*
> *Has groomed its wings*[48]
> *And many a times*
> *I have stirred this night*
> *Yearning for your arrival.*

Just then it started to rain heavily, and I added:

These days,
As snow and sleet mingle,
I spend my night waking,
Watching the morning frost;
Wondering whether
Your love too
Has grown cold.

The Law

That night he visited me again, and we talked at length of many things, when he said, "Would you feel betrayed when, after I have brought you to my place, I enter a monastery and become a Buddhist monk?" He spoke sadly, and I thought, *Why on earth has such a thought entered his mind? Can such a thing really be true?* Overcome with melancholy I could not keep myself from weeping.

Outside, the sleet rained down quietly.

I was so upset that I could not sleep at all, but the prince addressed me with tender words, pledging an undying love that would last until the life hereafter. And I thought, *His emotions are true enough, and he listens to me without becoming distracted. And I, in return, by way of showing my true affections for him, had made up my mind to join him at the palace. Yet if he now is to enter a monastery, I might just as well carry through my original intentions of becoming a nun myself.* Thinking of this made me even sadder, and all I could do was sob, unable to utter a single word.

Seeing me like this the prince composed an opening stanza:

> *Lovers' fancy of a moment*
> *Held us both throughout the night…*

And I completed it:

> *Tears came to their eyes,*
> *And all around was rain.*

The prince, too, seemed more dispirited than usual and talked of various things, though with little confidence. And when dawn finally broke he returned to the palace.

I spent the rest of the day in a state of confusion thinking, *Though I did not harbor any great expectations, it was to lift my gloom that I had made up my mind to join him at the palace. But what do I do when he now decides to enter a monastery?* And so I wrote to him:

> *How am I to live*
> *Without you in my world?*
> *On waking I cannot think.*
> *I wish they were only dreams.*

These are my true thoughts; how could you think of such a thing?

And in the margin I wrote:

> *We made our vows so earnestly,*
> *Yet must these vows now yield*
> *To just another commonplace*
> *In this changing world.*

I am so sad to think of it.

The prince read my letter and replied:

THE IZUMI SHIKIBU NIKKI

I had wanted to be the first to write you after our night together, but you beat me to it—

> *I want you to forget*
> *My talk of monasteries.*
> *Those sad things were only dreams,*
> *Dreamed in a night of dreams.*

You are impatient to immediately think the worst—

> *Only life is fickle:*
> *We know not how it will end.*
> *But promises shall endure*
> *Like the pine tree*
> *Along the coast at Suminoe.*[49]

O my beloved, I won't speak of it again. It's just another thing I brought upon myself, without being able to carry it through.

After that, I languished in a state of melancholy, unable to even breathe a sigh. I was making preparations to join the prince, when, at noon, the prince sent me another letter. And opening it, I found it contained another allusion to an old poem:

> *Oh, how I long for you,*
> *As if I had just seen you*
> *Like a Yamato* nadeshiko[50]
> *Growing in a country hedge.*

"Dear me! Isn't he head over heels!" I exclaimed despite myself. And so I replied with a line from the *Ise monogatari*:

> *If you love me,*
> *Come and see me,*
> *Even the gods*
> *Will not forbid*
> *Those who follow*
> *Love's pathway.*

The prince had to smile when he read the poem. And since the prince was lately in the habit of reading *sūtra* he wrote me the following poem:

THE IZUMI SHIKIBU NIKKI

*The gods may not forbit
Those who tread love's pathway,
But since I occupy
The Seat of the Law
I cannot presently leave it.*

I answered:

*In that case
I will come to you.
So that you may devote yourself
To the spread of the Law.*

Bamboo Joints

Once it snowed heavily and he sent me a poem attached to a branch covered with snow:

> *Snow falls,*
> *And on all the branches*
> *Plum flowers are in bloom,*
> *Though it is not yet spring.*

I wrote back:

> *Thinking the plum flowers were in bloom*
> *I broke the branch,*
> *And snow scattered like flowers.*

Early next morning he sent me another poem:

> *These winter nights*
> *Lovers keep vigil.*
> *Day dawned*
> *As I lay in my lonely bed*
> *Without having met you.*

I answered:

How right you are—

> *Chilled by the winter cold*
> *My eyes were frozen with tears;*
> *And so I waited for the break of dawn*
> *Amid the dark of night.*

Thus we spent our days, seeking to console each other through incoherent lines—yet how vain and fruitless!

I wondered what the prince must be thinking, for his words were so disheartening that even wrote, "Well, perhaps I am bound to soon end my days…"

So I wrote to him:

> *Is it just I who reminisces*
> *About our moments together,*
> *As people have done*
> *From generation to generation,*
> *Like the joints*
> *In a bamboo stalk?*

He replied:

> *I would not exist,*
> *Even for a moment*
> *In a world where sorrows*
> *Follow one another like the joints*
> *In a bamboo stalk.*

To the Palace

Though the prince had been troubling himself to find a suitable place to hide me, he reflected, *She is not used to such a life and would be embarrassed by it. For my part, I should be much rebuked. It is better if I go and bring her myself.*

And so, on the eighteenth of December, while the moon was out in full splendor, he visited me.

He casually said, "Well, let's go."

I thought that, as usual, it was only for the night. But when I got into the palanquin alone, he said, "Take a maid or the like with you. If you are willing we can talk quietly."

I thought to myself, *He has never before suggested I take a maid with me, even when we spent several night away. Can it be that he wants to bring me to the palace forthwith?* And so I did.

He did not bring me to the usual place, but to well-prepared rooms where I could freely be served by my maids. Now I was sure I had understood him, and thought, *He just brought me here without any ado. Still, I suppose it is better if people are taken unaware—my coming here will simply be a fait acompli.*

By now dawn had broken, and I sent my maid to go and collect the beauty chest containing my combs.

The prince was still in my room, so I instructed her not to raise the shutters. And though the dark was not frightful, it was nevertheless gloomy inside.

"I wish," said the prince noticing my discomfort, "to arrange that you shall live in the northern wing of my residence. This room is too much near the main hall and has no charm in it."

So we stayed inside with the shutters down and silently listened to what went on around us. And in the daytime we could hear the court ladies and cortiers of the prince's father, Emperor Reizei gathering outside, saying, "How is it that she has been brought here like this?"

The prince said: "It hurts me to think you might be disappointed, even though you have only just joined me here.

THE IZUMI SHIKIBU NIKKI

I said, "I rather fear the people around you might be disappointed if they see me at your side."

He laughed and said: "In all honesty, do take care of yourself while I am away at night. It would be untoward if, out of mere curiosity, some impertinent fellow happens to catch a glimpse of you. For the time being you can go to the quarters of the imperial wet nurse. People hardly drop by there at all. And I will meet you there again."

Court Life

After two days I was removed to the northern wing of the palace. The court ladies were astonished and ran and told the princess, who said, "Even without this event, the prince's conduct has been deplorable. But to bring someone here who is not even of high birth—it is too much to bear." But when she realized he might have brought me here because he favored me more than her, she could not brook me at all and grew more sullen than ever.

The prince, on his side, was embarrassed by it all. It pained him to hear the rumors that were being spread. He did not want to confront the opprobrium of his wife and those around him, and thus he stayed away from his wife's quarters and spent all his time in my quarters.

Talking through her tears the princess said to the prince, "All I hear is rumors. Why is that you did not tell me of your plan to bring her here? It isn't that I would have told you to desist. Yet you treat me like the first best commoner, so that now I am the laughingstock of the whole world. The humiliation is just too much to bear!"

The prince replied, "I brought her here to be my maid. So why all the fuss? Nor can you feign ignorance altogether. With you being so mad at me all the time, your chief maid has come to dislike me too. So I brought her here to help me with my hair. Indeed, feel free to use her yourself."

The prince's words only served to make the princess even more unhappy and she did not utter another word.

Thus the days passed and I became used to court life. I dressed his hair and served him in everything, not parting from his side for a moment. The prince visited his wife's quarters less and less, and the princess's grief knew no limits.

New Year

The year turned back and on the first day of the New Year, and a multitude of courtiers assembled to pay their respect to the emperor. The prince too was in attendance and looked young and handsome, far more so than the great number of noblemen who were there. He looked so dashing that I felt awkward with my own shabby appearance.

The court ladies of the princess sat down along the edge of the room, but weren't at all looking at the gathering, but making a terrible din, even poking holes in the paper windows, just to get a sight of "the prince's new fancy." It was unsightly in the extreme.

When it grew dark, the ceremony came to an end, and the emperor withdrew to the Southern Hall. To see him off, the nobles rose and then sat down again to partake in a musical entertainment with wind and string instruments. It was all so dazzling and colorful that I had to think of my own lonely and miserable life at home.

It was while I had been in the prince's service for some time that it came to the prince's notice that two of his menial servants had been slandering me. He said, "I am outraged to think that my wife should think so badly of her that even our menial servants are now badmouthing her," and from then on he hardly ever visited the princess's quarters again. It felt unbearable to think that the prince and the princess had thus been estranged from each other on my account, and I though, *What shall I do? What can I do? What else than devotedly follow the prince in the way he decides to handle this matter?*

The Princess Leaves

The princess's elder sister was engaged to the crown prince and just then was living with her parents.[51] She wrote to the princess:

How are you been? Is it true what people are saying? Even I feel treated like I'm less than a commoner lately. Please come to us during the night.

The princess thought, *Even if it isn't as bad as she says, what on earth is it that they are saying?* This made her feel only more miserable, and she wrote back to her sister:

I have received your letter. My husband and I have never

got on well, but recently a most dreadful thing has happened. I would really like to come home and see all the faces of the young princes, if only for a short while; it would very much console me. Please send someone out with a carriage to come and collect me. As long as I'm not here, I won't have to put up with this tedious talk.

Having dispatched her letter, the princess began to collect the articles for her return home. And ordering her servants to clean up her quarters, she said, "I plan to go and stay with my sister for a while. I cannot bear being here any longer. After all, it must be a burden for the prince too to have to come over here and visit me at my quarters." When she said this, all the court ladies who were present began to talk into her, saying things like, "This is unheard of! Did your ladyship know the people are making fun of the prince with all kinds of slander?" And, "When that woman came to live here at the palace, the prince went out of his way to go and fetch her—what an unseemly state of affairs!" And, "She lives in that room over there, and it seems the prince visits her three or five times a day!" And, "You should give him a proper scolding—that's what you should do!" And, "The prince just isn't showing you the respect your ladyship deserves!"

The princess was utterly mortified to hear her ladies-in-waiting talk hatefully of the prince in unison. She thought, *This is too much. I cannot bear this talk any longer. I need to get away from here!* And in her distress she cried out, "Please, sister, come and rescue me!"

Just then a man who turned out to be her older brother arrived and said, "I have come to collect you." And the princess thought, *Finally!*

Hearing that the princess's wet nurse had been instructed to clean up her ladyship's quarters, the house keeper flew into a panic and said to the prince, "It seems her ladyship the princess is getting ready to leave the palace. If your brother the crown prince hears of this there will be trouble! Please go to her and try and stop her!"

Overhearing this, I was heartbroken to think of the pain I had caused, but as it would be unseemly for me to interfere, I remained silent and just listened. I wanted to leave the room, so I wouldn't have to hear all this, but that too would have been deplorable, and so I just sat there, though the whole ordeal made me feel more wretched than ever.

When the prince entered his wife's quarters she acted as if nothing had happened. "Is this true?" the prince asked. "Is it true that you are going away to stay with your sister? Pray why did you not ask *me* to send for a carriage?"

But the princess merely answered, "Why should I? They already sent one for me." It was all she said.[52]

Glossary

daimyō: Feudal lord.

dera or *tera*: Temple.

hokku: Opening stanza of a Japanese orthodox collaborative linked poem.

hototogisu: Lesser cuckoo (*Cuculus poliocephalus*), a bird native to Japan.

karaginu: wide-sleeved jacket that reaches only to the waist. It is a component of the multi-layered Heian court costume known as *jūnihitoe* (twelve layers).

kagura: Type of Shintō ritual ceremonial dance.

kichō: A kind of screen used in upper-class houses.

misu:	Finer sort of *sudare* used in court or in Shintō shrine.
nagauta:	Lit. "long song;" a kind of traditional Japanese music which accompanies the *kabuki* theater.
rōnin:	Masterless samurai.
shōgun:	Hereditary military ruler during Japan's feudal era.
sudare:	Ancient ladies avoided men's eyes and always sat behind sudare (finely split bamboo curtain) through which they could look out without being seen.
tanka:	Thirty-one-syllable poem.
tachibana:	Species of citrus fruit native to Japan.
uchigi:	One of a series of robe layers typically worn as a component of the multi-layered Heian court costume known as *jūnihitoe* (twelve layers).
zuihitsu:	Genre of Japanese literature consisting of loosely connected personal essays and fragmented ideas that typically respond to the author's surroundings.

Notes

1. In Japanese poetry, Amida Buddha is often compared to the moon which rises over the mountains and lights the traveller's path.
2. Prince Tametaka, the third son of Emperor Reizei (950–1011). The prince died on June 13, 1002. Tametaka's affair with Izumi Shikibu caused a great scandal, as a result of which her husband divorced her and her family disowned her.
3. In those days noblemen's houses were surrounded with an embankment, instead of a wall.
4. Prince Atsumichi (981–1007), the fourth son of Emperor Reizei.
5. The *hototogisu* sings when the *tachibana* is in flower. In

this instance the *hototogisu* means the young prince. Thus there is a suggestion here if he chooses to take it.
6 An allusion to lines from the *Kokin wakarokujō*.
7 Ukon no Jō, an officer in the prince's bodyguard. He seems to have been an attendant of the late prince Tametaka, before he served the present prince.
8 Though, unlike her elder sisters, we do not know the name of Prince Atsumichi's consort, we know that she was the youngest daughter of Fujiwara Naritoki (941–995). She had married Prince Atsumichi after he had divorced his first wife, Yoriko, following the death of her father, Fujiwara Michitaka (953–995).
9 An allusion to lines from the *Gosen wakashū*.
10 The *hototogisu* sings with a low note in early spring, but when April has passed his voice grows clear and loud. It is a favorite singing bird in Japan.
11 Fujiwara Kinsue (957–1029), an uncle of the prince's mother.
12 Crown prince Okisada, the second son of Emperor Reizei, and the future Emperor Sanjō (976–1017).
13 An allusion to lines from the *Shūi wakashū*.
14 An allusion to lines from the *Ise monogatari*.

THE IZUMI SHIKIBU NIKKI

15 An allusion to lines from the *Haku shimonjū*.
16 An allusion to lines from the *Tsurayukishū*.
17 An allusion to lines from the *Kokin wakashū*.
18 Prime minister Fujiwara no Michinaga, the most powerful man of the age.
19 An allusion to lines from the *Kokin wakarokujō*.
20 An allusion to lines from the *Kokin wakashū*:

> *Were my heart to grow faithless,*
> *And beat for another man,*
> *May waves pass over the hill of pines,*
> *Where I wait for my beloved!*

In Japanese, the word *matsu* can equally mean "pine tree" or "wait" (though they are written with different Chinese characters).

21 An allusion to lines from the *Shūi wakashū*.
22 Another allusion to lines from the *Shūi wakashū*.
23 An allusion to lines from the *Kokin wakashū*.
24 The Festival of the stars, on the seventh day of the seventh month, when it was customary to write letters or pay visits in memory of the heavenly lovers.

25 An allusion to lines from the *Kokin wakarokujō*.
26 An allusion to lines from the *Kokin wakashū*.
27 The Ishiyama temple is located some five miles east of Kyoto, and commands a fine view of Lake Biwa.
28 The Ausaka barrier, situated just east of Kyoto, was one of the three (tax) barriers of Ausaka, Fuwa, and Suzuka. Much of the following poems are construed around a play on the word *au* (to meet).
29 This group of poems are based on a play on the homophones *Au michi*, "the road to Ōmi (also Aumi)," and *au michi*, or a "way to meet." Ōmi was the name of the province in which the Ishiyama temple and Lake Biwa were situated.
30 Uchide is the place of an ancient burial site, or *kofun*. They are allusions to the following lines from the *Kokin wakashū*:

> *Were all in this world of ours*
> *To cast their lives aside*
> *With every sorrow*
> *This vale of tears*
> *Would soon be leveled.*

31 An allusion to lines from the *Shūi wakashū*.

32 An allusion to lines from the *Kokin wakashū*.

33 An allusion to lines from the *Kiyotadashū*.

34 An allusion to lines from the *Kinyōwakashū*.

35 An allusion to lines from the *Goshūi wakashū*.

36 The Japanese lady in her dwelling where the light was softened by her window-panes of white silk, or her *sudare*, dwelt always in a sort of twilight probably very becoming to beauty.

37 An allusion to lines from the *Kokin wakashū*.

38 An allusion to lines from the *Kokin wakarokujō*.

39 In autumn the leaves of the spindle tree become purple or red, and they are so pretty that people call them "mountain brocade."

40 According to an ancient fable, En no Gyōja, a great magician, summoned the goddess of Mount Katsuragi to build a stone bridge at Kume near Mount Katsuragi in the province of Yamato. The goddess was very shy and, working only at night, never showed herself in front of others. The magician grew angry with her, and punished her by unveiling her, causing the bridge only to be completed halfway.

41 An allusion to lines from her own *Izumi Shikibushū*.
42 The godless month—October, so called because in that month all the gods left their abodes and went to the high plain of heaven to hold counsel together.
43 Shikibu and her contemporaries believed in lucky and unlucky directions; those who went in an unlucky direction might have some unfortunate incident.
44 An allusion to lines from the *Kokin wakashū*.
45 In 997 Izumi Shikibu had given birth to Koshikibu no Naishi (who would also become a poetess and court lady). The father was Tachibana Michisada, to whom Shikibu was married when she began an affair with the late prince Tametaka.
46 An allusion to lines from the *Kokin wakashū*.
47 An allusion to lines from the *Kokin wakarokujō*.
48 An allusion to lines from the *Kokin wakashū*.
49 Another allusion to lines from the *Kokin wakashū*.

A long time has passed,
Even from where I am standing now;
How many generations
Has that princess pine

THE IZUMI SHIKIBU NIKKI

> *Stood on the banks*
> *Of Suminoe.*

The pine tree at Suminoe was famed for its age.

50 Another allusion to lines from the *Kokin wakashū:*

> *Aah, how I long for you*
> *Even now I want to meet her,*
> *That girl,*
> *(in the bloom of her life)*
> *Like a Yamato nadeshiko,*
> *Growing in some fence,*
> *Of a mountain village.*

Yamato nadeshiko (Japanese pink); the homonym means "the caressed girl of Yamato."

51 Fujiwara Naritoki's eldest daughter, Seishi, alternatively, Sukeko (972–1025), who went on to marry Emperor Sanjō (then crown prince Okisada) one year after his succession to the throne in 1011. By then Sanjō had already married Kenshi (the daughter of Seishi's cousin, Regent Fujiwara Michinaga).

52: In a final note, Shikubu comments that, "The words in the princess's letter, as well as the remarks by her ladies-in-waiting are not what they actually said, but written down in this book by me so as to resembly what they might have said or written."

A NOTE ON THE TRANSLATORS

Annie Shepley Ōmori (1856–1943) was an American artist and activist. Having studied art under Harry Siddons Mowbray in New York, and under Jules Joseph Lefebvre and Lucien Simon in Paris, she established her own art studios in New York and Connecticut, where, for the next three decades, she worked as a portrait painter and children's book illustrator.

It was during this period that she met the twenty-years-younger Hyōzō Ōmori, who had come to the United States as a YMCA exchange student. They married in 1907 and together moved to Japan, where they established the Yūrinen settlement house to provide educational and recreational opportunities to the poor in Tokyo. As such they became prominent leaders in the Japanese playground movement.

After her husband's death, in 1913, Shepley stayed in Japan continued running the center. And it was during this period that, together with the Japanese scholar of English literature, Kōchi Doi, she translated the diaries of Murasaki Shikibu, Izumi Shikibu, and Sugawara no Takasue no Musume.

Kōchi Doi (1886–1979) studied English literature and classic Japanese at Tokyo Imperial University. Following his graduation, he did research in France, England, and Italy. On his return to Japan he taught at a number of universities, introducing the English romanticism of James Joice, D.H. Lawrence, and Aldous Huxley. He also pursued his study of classical Japanese literature, the comparative study of mythology, as well as Eastern and Western literature. In 1949, after a distinguished career of various professorships, he became a member of the Japan Academy.

Amy Lawrence Lowell (1874–1925) was an American poet. Born into a wealthy Boston family, she was the sister of astronomer Percival Lowell, educator and legal scholar Abbott Lawrence Lowell, and early activist for prenatal care Elizabeth Lowell Putnam. She was the great-grandchild of John Lowell.

Though she did not enjoy a formal education herself, Lowell was a voracious reader and traveler. And it was whilst in Europe that, in 1902, she saw a performance by the Italian actresss Eleonora Duse, and was inspired to become a poet, publishing her first collection in 1912 under the title *A Dome of Many-Coloured Glass*. That same year, she traveled to England with her partner, Ada Dwyer Russel, to come under the spell of the Imagist movement of the expatriate American poet Ezra Pound.

An inveterate smoker of cigars, Lowell died in 1925 of a cerebral hemorrhage. One year later she was posthumously awarded the Pulitzer Prize for Poetry.

ALSO PUBLISHED BY TOYO PRESS

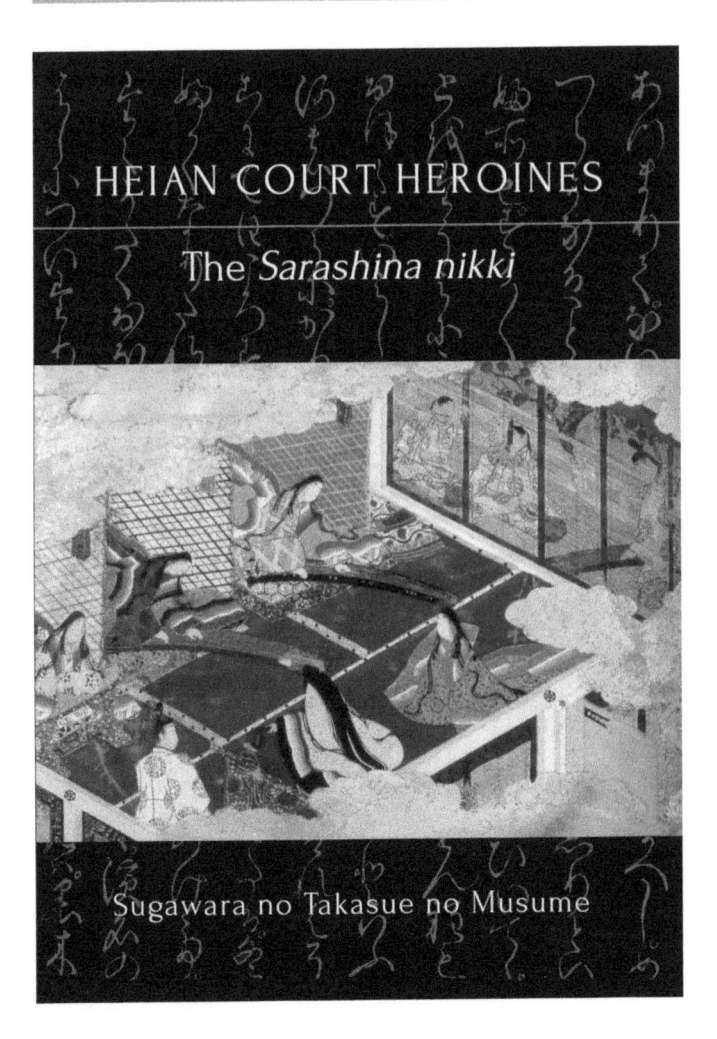

HEIAN COURT HEROINES

The *Sarashina nikki*

Sugawara no Takasue no Musume

ALSO PUBLISHED BY TOYO PRESS

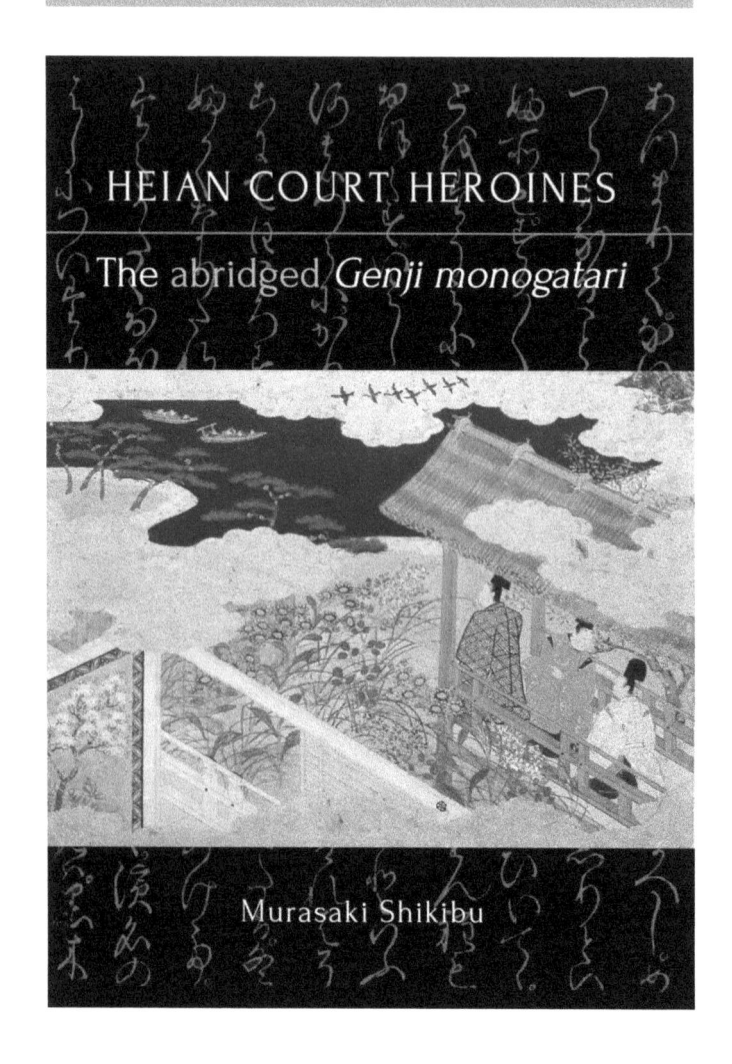

HEIAN COURT HEROINES

The abridged *Genji monogatari*

Murasaki Shikibu

TOYO PRess
Explore Dream Discover

Editorial supervision: William de Lange.
Book and cover design: Chōkei Studios.
The typefaces used are Cardo and Forum.
Printing and binding: IngramSpark.

Lightning Source UK Ltd.
Milton Keynes UK
UKHW040756070222
398308UK00001B/148